——— LOST LINES: ———
EASTERN

N I G E L   W E L B O U R N

IAN ALLAN
Publishing

C O N T E N T S

First published 1995
ISBN 0 7110 2383 2

Published by Ian Allan Publishing an imprint of Ian Allan Ltd, Terminal House,
Station Approach, Shepperton, Surrey TW17 8AS;
and printed by Ian Allan Printing Ltd, Coombelands House, Coombelands Lane,
Addlestone, Weybridge, Surrey KT15 1HY.

ACKNOWLEDGEMENTS
I would like to thank all those who helped me with this book.
In particular, I would like to thank my parents whose patience and understanding when I was
younger allowed me to visit so many lines that are now closed.
I would also like to thank all those courteous and helpful railwaymen and women who once
worked on the lines mentioned in this book.

Nigel P. Welbourn DIP TP, DIP TS, MRTPI, FRGS.

Cover photos courtesy Colour-Rail

Introduction

The Eastern Region is the fourth book in the 'Lost Lines' series. A cross-section of closed lines has been selected for this volume, for their regional interest and for their wider historical and geographical associations.

In 1923, by amalgamation of smaller companies, the railways of Great Britain were divided into the 'big four': the London & North Eastern Railway (LNER), the London Midland & Scottish Railway (LMS), the Great Western Railway (GWR) and the Southern Railway (SR). When these private companies were nationalised on 1 January 1948, the new organisation called 'British Railways' was divided into six regions for management purposes. A separate Eastern Region was established, the others being Scottish, London Midland, Southern, Western and North Eastern.

Although there had already been some closures, at their formation the six regions covered one of the most comprehensive railway networks in the world. Yet it was clear, even then, that the changing trends in economic and travel patterns were no longer reflected in the distribution of lines. The problem was compounded in that after heavy World War 2 use, the equipment on many lines was life-expired. Thus it was that the railways at Nationalisation had extensive arrears of both maintenance and investment.

The ever increasing inroads of the car and the lorry meant that financially the railways were no longer in a particularly sound position and British Railways fell ever deeper into debt. As a consequence, in the 1960s notice was served that the complete railway network, which had survived relatively intact until that time, would be scrutinised as never before. The financial contribution of individual lines was to be examined and it was clear, from the then somewhat stringent methods of accountancy, that many would be unlikely to survive on a purely commercial basis. In a surprisingly short time the system was reduced in size. By the 1970s, when the brake was eventually applied on closures, about 8,000 miles over the whole system had been lost, a length of closed line equal to the diameter of the world.

In the knowledge that change was inevitable, in the 1960s I started to record my travels by train. Starting first in the Eastern Region I eventually covered, with a few short exceptions, every passenger railway line on each of the six regions. The railway network is now much smaller than when I first set out and in fact the Eastern Region itself was abandoned after about four decades of geographical division in favour of other methods of organisation. My subsequent visits to lines closed show that much still survives. Indeed, the earthworks and structures of abandoned lines have their own fascination, lost at present, but certainly not forgotten.

Above: Map of the Regional Boundaries 1958.
Ian Allan Library

1 Historical perspective

England's oldest recorded town, Colchester, was located to the south of the Eastern Region (ER). Railways from London to such market towns formed the basis of much of the region, but the industrial northern parts and associated links provided a more lucrative market for the early railways. Later smaller independent railways in the region were absorbed by two railway companies in particular, the Great Eastern Railway (GER) and the Great Northern Railway (GNR). Indeed the Eastern Region for much of its existence, after losing the Great Central main line and before absorbing the North Eastern Region, primarily covered the former lines of the GER and the GNR.

One of the main constituents was the Great Eastern Railway which began as the Eastern Counties Railway and merged with four others in 1862. As its name implied, the railway covered the eastern counties of East Anglia and because of its vast agricultural freight it was sometimes nicknamed 'The Swedey'. The financial returns from many of the rural areas that it served could not justify vast engineering works, yet, although many of its lines were relatively economically constructed, the stations were often particularly fine. The London area was a sharp contrast to the sparse population in some of the rural areas and the most intensive steam suburban service in the world developed from Liverpool Street. The railway also had royal connections. It served the royal estate at Sandringham and its livery, a Royal Blue, dated back to a single engine and arch painted in this colour for Queen Victoria's opening of Epping Forest. Indeed the pre-World War 1 Royal Blue of its main line locomotives was perpetuated to the blue of the Eastern Region.

Below: In sharp contrast to the vast scale of Liverpool Street were a number of rural halts. This view of Ashdon Halt, between Bartlow and Saffron Walden, was taken on 22 March 1958 with the 4.6pm to Audley End being pushed by No 69651. *J. Spencer Gilks*

The largest constituent railway was the former Great Northern Railway which came into being in 1846 and ran from its King's Cross terminus in London, north along its fine main line to Doncaster, to form the southern part of the East Coast main line to Scotland. To some extent the railway concentrated on its long distance services to the north — at the expense of some of its other local services. It was the first railway in the country to run dining-cars, its somersault signals were a distinctive feature and its green dome-less engines were particularly fine. Nevertheless a number of suburban services and

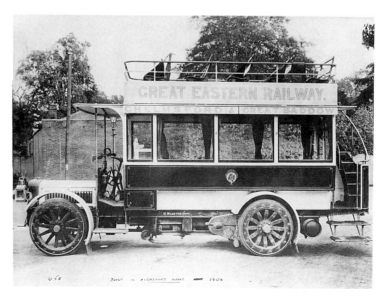

Above: One of the Great Eastern's premier routes was from Liverpool Street to Cromer. This view of Cromer High shows 'Claud Hamilton' class 4-4-0 No 1897 at the station in the early part of this century. A 'T19' class 2-4-0 stands to the right. *Locomotive Publishing Company*

Rght: The Great Eastern Railway ran an integrated transport service with buses running to a number of non-rail-served villages. This bus, built at Stratford Works in the early 1900s, ran from Chelmsford to Great Baddow. *Ian Allan Library*

many of its stations, King's Cross excepted, were functional rather than opulent. Many of the secondary lines of the Great Northern Railway have since disappeared, but its main line with its extensive engineering works stretching to the north and capable today of high speed running is a monument to the foresight of this railway.

At first the Eastern Region operated the former Great Central main line as far as Yorkshire and this connected with other ER routes in that area.

However, in later changes, the bulk of the Great Central main line was removed from the Eastern Region and placed in the London Midland Region and is therefore included in the LMR volume in this series.

The region embraced a number of other smaller former independent railways. The London Tilbury & Southend Railway (LT&S) ran from its attractive terminus at London Fenchurch Street to the towns suggested by its name. The routes became an eastern

Above: A Stirling 8ft Single No 665 departs from Boston in Lincolnshire. *Ian Allan Library*

Left: This view of a 'J6' class No 4220 was taken between Braceborough Spa and Essendine with a Bourne-Essendine train on 9 July 1949 on one of the many ex-GNR secondary routes to disappear. *P. Wells*

Right: Many lines, including some in the LMR, acted as connections from the Midlands to the Lincolnshire coast. This is a view of 'B1' No 61390 running through the derelict former GNR Lowesby station with a Mablethorpe to Leicester train on 27 August 1960. *J. Spencer Gilks*

Below: Class 20s Nos 20068 and 20067 pass a fine somersault distant signal at Barkston East with an eastbound passenger train to the Lincolnshire coast on Bank Holiday Monday, 26 May 1980. Mercifully some services to the coast still survive. *D. Tewson*

extremity of the LMS before passing more logically to the ER. They have not become substantial lost lines, except the branch to Tilbury Riverside. There were also some short sections of line, including the Mid-Suffolk and Colne Valley lines that had remained independent up to the LNER grouping.

The Eastern Region also inherited a number of joint lines including the Great Northern & Great Eastern Joint line which ran for well over 100 miles from Huntingdon, via Spalding, Lincoln and Gainsborough, to Black Carr Junction just south of Doncaster. Yet the best known former joint line to be run by ER was the Midland & Great Northern Joint Railway (M&GN). This was a self-contained system that ran eastward from Bourne and Peterborough, through the fens, to Norwich and the Norfolk coast. Later agreements with the Great Eastern Railway resulted in coastal lines being constructed between

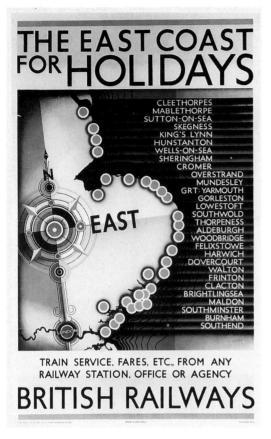

THE EAST COAST FOR HOLIDAYS

CLEETHORPES
MABLETHORPE
SUTTON-ON-SEA
SKEGNESS
KING'S LYNN
HUNSTANTON
WELLS-ON-SEA
SHERINGHAM
CROMER
OVERSTRAND
MUNDESLEY
GRT: YARMOUTH
GORLESTON
LOWESTOFT
SOUTHWOLD
THORPENESS
ALDEBURGH
WOODBRIDGE
FELIXSTOWE
HARWICH
DOVERCOURT
WALTON
FRINTON
CLACTON
BRIGHTLINGSEA
MALDON
SOUTHMINSTER
BURNHAM
SOUTHEND

EAST

N

LONDON

TRAIN SERVICE, FARES, ETC., FROM ANY
RAILWAY STATION, OFFICE OR AGENCY

BRITISH RAILWAYS

Above: This former British Railways poster shows
that most East Coast resorts were once served by rail.
Of the 29 destinations shown on this poster, no less
than 17 still retain their rail services. *Courtesy NRM*

Cromer and Mundesley and between Yarmouth and
Lowestoft. These lines helped to integrate the M&GN
system into the GER, but failed to save it from an
early closure.

From 1 January 1923, with the exception of eventually the LT&S section, the railways mentioned above
were merged into the London & North Eastern
Railway. This company's boundary was rather greater
than the Eastern Region, running the East Coast main
line to Scotland and with extremities of the system
extending to Mallaig, Lossiemouth and Liverpool;
locations way beyond the eventual Eastern Region.
However, for administrative purposes, the southern
area of the LNER consisted of the former GNR, GER
and GCR lines, an area not dissimilar to the eventual

ER.

Competition between the LNER's East Coast main
line and the LMS's West Coast main line, between
London and Scotland are legendary, but the East
Coast main line was particularly noted for speed with
Sir Nigel Gresley's 'A4' Mallard No 4468 reaching
126 mph on this line near Essendine in July 1938. A
record for speed by a steam locomotive unbeaten to
this day.

Then came World War 2. Whilst petrol rationing
for cars extended the life of some branch lines, World
War 2 resulted in a lack of investment that was to
speed the demise of many lines in later years.
Although the East Coast main line recovered to provide fast services with romance and panache, the
LNER was unkindly labelled by some as the 'Late and
Never Early Railway'. It was also not particularly
financially successful, being the least profitable of the
'big four' railways and there was general relief at its
nationalisation in 1948.

Thus the Eastern Region came into being. This
broadly included much of the London & North
Eastern Railway to the south of the Humber estuary.
The house colour selected was a form of the Royal
Blue not unlike that of the Great Eastern Railway.
From 1958 and for many years the region divided the
routes on its maps broadly between the Great Eastern
and Great Northern lines, whilst the former Great
Central lines were shown on Eastern Region maps
clearly as 'Other Regions Lines' in a faded blue, even
after they had been transferred to the London
Midland Region.

The ER was in the forefront of conversion to diesel
traction and can be credited with improvements to its
main lines, including introducing the 'Deltic' fleet to
the East Coast main line, completing the Essex coast
electrification and improving the lines to Cambridge
and Norwich. Regardless of the wider implications,
the Beeching Report in 1963 identified many secondary lines in the region for closure. Vast areas of
East Anglia and Lincolnshire, particularly lines to the
coast, which had busy summer peaks, but sparse winter traffic, were identified for closure. Vigorous fights
were put up in many areas; indeed in November 1967
the region was unique in sacking its Chairman and
General Manager, Mr Gerard Fiennes, for his outspo-
ken views on the running of railways. Nevertheless
closures continued until the 1970s when the brake
was put on further cuts and a network emerged that
remains not dissimilar to that of today.

The ER eventually merged with the North Eastern
Region (NER) before being disbanded in favour of
other forms of management structures. For the purposes of this series of books the ER is considered as
it existed for many years, after loss of the GCR main
line, but prior to merger with the NER.

2 Geography of the region

The Eastern Region, for much of its existence, broadly included those lines east of the East Coast main line from London and the Thames estuary in the south, to Doncaster and the Humber estuary in the north. It included all lines in the East Anglian counties and in Lincolnshire. As originally constituted it also ran the Great Central main line. Nevertheless in the 1950s this route was transferred to the London Midland Region, with the exception of an area from near Chesterfield to near Penistone which remained in the Eastern Region, together with other lines in the Sheffield area.

The region included the suburban lines of the former Great Eastern Railway around London and other suburban lines associated with the Great Northern Railway. Its prestige route was the East Coast main line via Peterborough to Doncaster, after which it entered the NER. Other main routes ran to Harwich, Norwich and Cambridge. The region served the south Yorkshire areas of Sheffield, Rotherham and Barnsley, but as can be seen many of the great areas of population and industry were not served by this region.

With notable exceptions, such as the eastern flanks of the Pennines, the bulk of the geography of the region was not unduly precipitous so that, again with some exceptions, there were few huge engineering structures. The Lincolnshire Wolds were in contrast to the flat Fens, but typically in the eastern counties the gradients of many lines reflected the undulating countryside. In East Anglia there were only two tunnels of any length and equally few vast viaducts, but there were numerous substantial bridges, including some over navigable rivers.

The east coast ports, including Tilbury, Maldon, Brightlingsea, Harwich, Felixstowe, Ipswich, Lowestoft, Yarmouth, Wells-next-the-Sea, King's Lynn, Boston and Immingham were all served by the region. Equally, an abundance of cathedral cities included Norwich, Ely, Peterborough and Lincoln.

With the exception of the northwest area the region was not predominantly industrial. This was marked to some extent that in travelling westwards it was clear that you moved from the shiny blue totems of the Eastern to the darker and dirtier London Midland muddy maroon totems. To a child living in Suffolk this gave the Eastern Region an air of friendly rurality compared with the dark satanic mills of areas served by the London Midland Region.

The Eastern Region also served the east coast and its holiday resorts, the larger ones being Southend, Clacton, Felixstowe, Lowestoft, Yarmouth, Skegness and Cleethorpes, all of which have retained rail services. On the other hand the more modest Brightlingsea, Aldeburgh, Mundesley, Wells, Hunstanton and Mablethorpe have all lost their services.

The region served vast agricultural tracts and for many years agricultural freight was an important source of income. The sugar beet season in East Anglia provided additional revenue that kept a number of freight spurs open long after the rest of the line had closed to passenger traffic. In contrast the lines into London, particularly from suburban Essex and Hertfordshire, were and still are, some of the busiest commuter routes in the world. Indeed, the problem at Liverpool Street was never so much with contraction, but how to handle the ever growing peak flow of passengers.

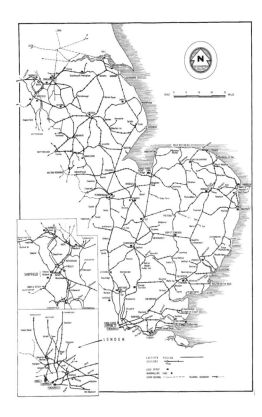

Above: The Eastern Region. *Author's Collection*

③ The Pally passengers

Alexandra Palace was largely built by 1873 and was north London's answer to the Crystal Palace. The opening of the 'Ally Pally' as it was, and still is, affectionately known, was co-ordinated with the opening of a railway to convey passengers up the ridge of Muswell Hill to a rear entrance of the Palace. The Muswell Hill Railway (the word 'Palace' was later included in its name) opened a 1³/₄-mile branch from Park Junction, near Highgate, to Alexandra Palace. There were eventually two intermediate stations and a substantial viaduct between Cranley Gardens, where the serial killer Dennis Nilsen once lived, and Alexandra Palace. The station at Alexandra Palace was built in a style and materials to reflect the Palace itself and direct access was provided into the Palace from the station.

Traffic was brisk on opening in May 1873, but the line's major source of income was the Palace so when fire caused its temporary closure the following month, the line was also forced to close. Indeed enforced temporary closures occurred after half a dozen other incidents right up to the 1950s. The line was taken over by the GNR in 1911 and traffic was heavy when functions were being held, whilst in 1936

Left: A former Great Northern Railway Class N2 0-6-2T runs round its train at Alexandra Palace shortly before closure of the line to passenger traffic. *Ian Allan Library*

Below: A similar view taken in August 1994. Much of the station area at Alexandra Palace has been given over to a car park, but the booking hall remains. *Author*

Alexandra Palace also became the first television centre.

When the line passed to the LNER they were unable to afford electrification and explored the possibility of working with the then London Passenger Transport Board, which was embarking on a government-assisted programme of improvements to the underground system. It looked as if the Alexandra Palace line would become an electrified branch of the Northern Line, together with the link to Finsbury Park. Improvements to the signalling were made and substantial cabling and ducting was laid in anticipation of electrification of the branch.

Progress was halted on the outbreak of

World War 2, but after that the situation changed. A decline in the popularity of the Palace and in traffic on the line meant that not only was the electrification scheme not proceeded with, but before long the branch itself was proposed for closure. The line closed to passengers in July 1954 (freight ran to Muswell Hill until June 1956 and to Cranley Gardens until May 1957), thereby missing an opportunity to become part of the Northern Line.

Although the branch has been built upon in one part, there have been constant rumours of a revival and conversion into part of the London rail system. The Palace was again struck by fire in 1980, the railway not being affected for once because it had long since closed. It was generally considered that this was the end, but against all the odds the Palace was reopened, an omen perhaps for the future of the railway.

Above : Alexandra Palace viewed on 5 May 1956. It is clear that, as today, intending passengers simply had to walk the line!
A. A. Jackson

Left: The former entrance and booking hall at Alexandra Palace station photographed in August 1972. *J. N. Young*

Opposite top: The same view in August 1994 after Alexandra Palace station had been restored and put to local community use. *Author*

Opposite : Map of Alexandra Palace branch 1894. *Crown Copyright*

Today the station at Alexandra Palace has been well restored and cleaned and is in community use. The surface station at Highgate also exists, having been rendered redundant by the Northern Line tunnelling underneath, thereby providing the present tube station at a lower level. The 'Ally Pally' line is used as a footpath for much of its length. This includes the viaduct around Muswell Hill town centre and spectacular views over London can be seen from this structure. Furthermore a short section from Park Junction, now known as Highgate Woods Sidings, remains in use in connection with the Highgate Underground Depot.

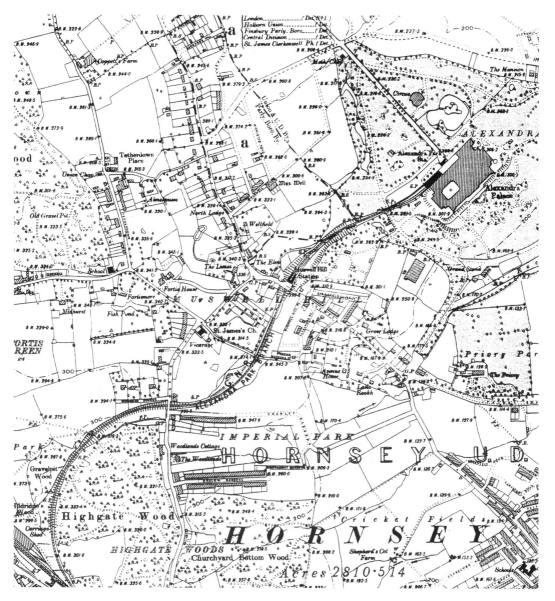

13

Left: The substantial viaduct on the line at Muswell Hill which in 1994 provided a home under its arches for many small scale industries as well as a footpath along the overgrown track above. *Author*

Centre: Cranley Gardens station in June 1954. This station was added to the branch after the line's original opening as a result of development in the area. Notwithstanding this, a country branch atmosphere is clearly apparent from this view. *J. N. Young*

Left: The original station at Highgate lies directly above the present tube station. In 1994 the former GNR trackbed had been covered over in an effort to prevent water seepage into the underground station below. *Author*

4 Back to Buntingford

The Ware, Hadham & Buntingford Railway opened its line in July 1863. This ran from a junction on the Broxbourne and Hertford branch to the north of St Margaret's. The branch crossed the River Lea and associated watercourses no less than eight times, travelling at first in a north-easterly direction to Hadham. It then turned north, running in total some 13¾ miles over undulating Hertfordshire countryside to reach Buntingford. The Romans had found little difficulty in crossing this area and equally the

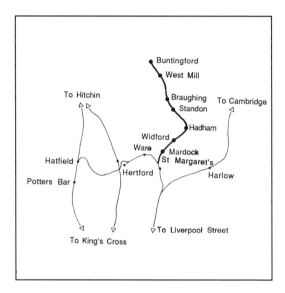

Table II—continued   **BUNTINGFORD and ST. MARGARET'S**

Miles		Week Days																				Sundays			
		a.m	a.m	a.m	a.m	a.m	a.m	a.m	a.m	a.m	a.m	p.m	p.m	p.m	p.m	p.m	p.m	p.m	p.m	p.m	p.m	p.m	a.m	p.m	p.m	p.m
				EZ		S	S	EZ	S		S	E		p.m	p.m	p.m	p.m	E	S	E	E	S		Y		
—	Buntingford.........dep	6 10	7 29	9 12	..	8 12	8 59	8 59	9 20	..	1056	1114	..	1 28	2 26	2 45	4 3	..	5 17	6 56	7 47	7 56	8 23	..	8 32	6 26	8 20
1½	West Mill.............	6 13	7 35	9 15	..	8 15	2 9	2 9	9 23	..	1059	1117	..	1 31	2 29	2 48	4 6	..	5 20	6 57	7 7	7 59	8 26	..	8 35	6 29	8 23
3½	Braughing...........	6 18	7 40	9 20	..	8 20	2 7	2 7	9 28	..	11 4	1122	..	1 36	2 34	2 53	4 11	..	5 25	7 4	7 15	8 4	8 31	..	8 40	6 31	8 28
4½	Standon...............	6 21	7 43	9 23	..	8 23	9 10	9 10	9 31	..	11 7	1125	..	1 39	2 37	2 56	4 14	..	5 32	7 7	7 18	7 34		..	8 43	6 34	8 31
8	Hadham	6 29	7 52	9 31	..	8 31	9 18	9 18	9 39	..	1115	1133	..	1 47	2 45	3 4	4 22	..	5 44	7 15	7 26	8 15	8 42	..	8 51	6 42	8 39
10	Widford	6 34	7 55	9 36	..	8 36	9 23	9 23	9 44	..	1120	1138	..	1 52	2 50	9 9	4 27	..	5 49	7 20	7 31	8 20	8 47	..	8 55	6 47	8 44
11	Mardock.............	6 37	7 59	9 39	..	8 39	9 26	9 26	9 47	..	1123	1141	..	1 55	2 53	12 4	4 30	..	5 52	7 23	7 34	8 23	8 50	..	8 59	6 50	8 47
13½	St. Margaret's......arr	6 43	7 55	9 45	..	8 45	9 32	9 32	9 53	..	1129	1147	..	2 1	2 59	3 18	4 36	..	5 58	7 29	7 40	8 29	8 56	..	9 5	6 56	8 53
32½ 10	London (L. St.) ...arr	7 43	8 39	9 33	..	9 39	1027	1039	1113	..	1237	1237	..	3 24	4 4	255	5 4	..	7 7	8 40	9 17	9 34	1010	..	1014	7 46	10 2

     S Arr. 4 minutes *earlier*.   **M** Except Saturdays   **S** Saturdays only   **E** Arr. 5 minutes *earlier*   **Y** Through Train
     between Buntingford and Liverpool Street until 4th September   **Z** Through Train between Buntingford and Liverpool Street

topography resulted in few extensive engineering works on the railway. From its title it could be assumed that the line ran from Ware, but opposition from landowners in this area, rather than physical

Above: The timetable for July 1955.

Below: Hadham station on 22 August 1964. The design and disposition of the buildings were very similar at a number of stations on the branch. *Ian Allan Library*

Above: The decayed and rotting shell of Braughing signal-box prior to being blown down by gales after this view was taken in February 1983. *Author*

Left: One of the original oil lamps from Braughing station, at last converted to electricity as this view taken in the summer of 1994 shows. *Author*

Below: One of the attractive wooden station buildings at Braughing in July 1994. Similar sheds were built at other stations on the line. *Author*

Left: A DMU has arrived at Buntingford station on 23 April 1962.
Ian Allan Library

Below: Buntingford signalbox. Note the window at the left hand end of the box to give visibility around the water tank.
A. Lawrence

problems, prevented direct connection to that town and forced the branch to connect to the main line at St Margaret's.

Although in later years commuting developed to London, the original purpose of the line was to alleviate Buntingford's further decline as the town had fallen between the Great Northern and Great Eastern main lines. Indeed under earlier plans it was intended that the branch would extend northward to join the Cambridge line near Shelford, but opposition meant that this plan, which would have seen the branch become a useful diversionary loop, was thrown out by Parliament. As it was, the serving of this relatively small settlement resulted in the branch being a risky

financial proposition from the start and the Great Eastern Railway soon took over the line. However, traffic on the line grew, together with local passenger services and commuting to London and a number of through trains were provided to the City. There was also considerable agricultural freight and the flour

---

Below: The distinctive steep gables to the exterior of Buntingford station in July 1994. *Author*

---

mill at Standon at one time contributed three freight trains a day to the line.

The introduction of diesel trains in 1959 and the closure of the small Buntingford engine shed were the only significant later investments and changes on the branch. Sadly it resulted in the discontinuance of through trains on to the adjoining electrified lines to London, which in turn saw a further decline in the passenger fortunes of the branch. There was little other investment in the route and the original oil lights remained on most of the platforms until the line's closure. Sunday services ceased in the autumn of 1955 and from 1960 services became mainly peak hour. Passenger services ceased in November 1964 and freight in September the following year.

Ever diminishing traces remain of the line itself, although a number of buildings have endured, including the main station buildings at Buntingford, albeit currently in a deteriorating condition. At Braughing all the station buildings also existed in a state of continuing dereliction for many years. The signalbox blew down in the first of the strong winds of the 1980s, but the other buildings have since been restored. This was an attractive little line, a real GER time capsule. It served this part of Hertfordshire faithfully, untouched essentially since it opened, but remaining still in the affections of people in the area.

5 Stour Valley stopping trains

The route from Marks Tey, on the main line south of Colchester, to Shelford, on the main line south of Cambridge, provided a useful secondary cross-country line between Cambridge and the east coast.

The 43¾-mile line developed in three sections. The first part constructed was from Marks Tey to Sudbury which opened in July 1849. This section contained the largest brick viaduct in East Anglia, the sturdy double-track width 32-arched structure being over 1,000ft long and rising to 70ft over the River Colne at Chappel. The second section opened from Cambridge to Haverhill in June 1865 and the link that connected

this northern section to Sudbury opened two months later. Together the three links formed a through route between Cambridge and Colchester.

A number of lines connected with this

cross-country route. A 16⅛-mile link opened from Long Melford to Bury St Edmunds via Lavenham in August 1865, whilst a 7¼-mile link was also provided from November 1865 between Bartlow and Audley End via Saffron Walden. Between Chappel & Wakes Colne and Haverhill once ran the 19⅛-mile Colne Valley & Halstead Railway. This line opened from Chappel to Halstead — at one time the latter was an important silk weaving town — in April 1860 and was extended to Haverhill by May 1863. The line never formed part of the GER, remaining an independent company until the Grouping in 1923. Whilst in practice the line could have competed with the GER, as it provided an even more direct line between Cambridge and Colchester, it was of course entirely dependent on the GER for the bulk of its traffic.

Above: A special train pulled by a BTH Type 1 diesel with a vintage collection of coaches passes Earls Colne station. *S. Creer*

Centre: Although actually near Castle Hedingham, one of the platforms on the preserved Colne Valley Railway has been named as 'Halstead' as this view taken in August 1994 shows. *Author*

Right: Halstead station looking towards Marks Tey with some evidence of freight activity in the yard in the late 1950s. *Real Photographs Co*

Left: Once the Stour Valley line was truncated at Sudbury the station here was allowed to fall into an appalling state of disrepair before its eventual demolition, as this view taken on 5 June 1973 shows. *G. D. King*

Below: Two Cravens-built DMUs meet at Long Melford. The line branching off to the right in the background is the Long Melford-Bury St Edmunds branch which had recently been closed when this view was taken in 1961. *M. Edwards*

Above left: Long Melford station, with few passengers, taken from the train on 7 April 1964. Removal of the signal for the Bury route is to be noted. *Author*

Above right: Cavendish station taken from the train on 7 April 1964. Note the rather useless fire buckets! *Author*

Below: Long Melford station buildings, happily restored in August 1994. *Author*

After World War 2 the network of lines saw a gradual decline in both freight, as the textile industry declined, and passenger traffic. Although the lines provided some useful long distance routes and diesel trains were introduced in 1959, trains stopped at the many stations which made the alternative line via Ipswich and Bury St Edmunds more attractive to long distance travellers.

The Colne Valley was the first line to close,

Left: Map of the two stations at Haverhill 1928.
Crown Copyright

Above: The design of the waiting room at Clare station was very similar to that at Cavendish and a number of others on the line. This view at Clare, which is now a country park, shows that what has remained of the Stour Valley line will now hopefully be preserved for the future.
Author

Right: The standard Eastern Region Royal Blue with white lettering enamel name board outside Haverhill station on 18 February 1967, a month before the line closed.
G. R. Mortimer

although its own station in Haverhill had closed to passengers as far back as 1924; the last passenger train ran at the end of December 1961. Freight continued to run on the southern section until April 1965. Other connections to the Stour Valley line were also early casualties. The link from Long Melford to Bury St Edmunds closed in April 1961 and that from Bartlow, through Saffron Walden, to Audley End closed in September 1964. The final closure came with the long section north from Sudbury to Shelford

Above: Haverhill North was the ex-GER station in the town in 1950. The station has subsequently been demolished, but the site remained in 1994 undeveloped and even the metal kerb which once bounded the footpath to the right of this view remains amongst the dereliction. *Real Photographs Co*

Below: Bartlow station was the junction for the link line via Saffron Walden to Audley End. Here Cambridge and Colchester trains pass on 7 July 1956 hauled by 'J15s' 0-6-0s Nos 65390 and 65468. The location is now a garden. *H. C. Casserley*

via Haverhill closing in March 1967. The diary records a journey on the last train:

> *4 March, 1967: Went on last train from Haverhill to Cambridge and then last train from Cambridge to Sudbury. Packed both ways. Two coffins were seen (and lots of March hares in the fields), but as the paper said it was more like a carnival than a funeral. Detonators at all stations, fireworks and bonfires. Went to Sudbury a few weeks later and the track was already rusted over.*

Protest, which included well over 1,000 written objections, resulted in the section from Marks Tey to Sudbury being retained, including the section over the Chappel Viaduct. Although all the other routes have closed, a section of the Colne Valley railway has been reopened at Castle Hedingham, with plans to extend to Halstead, whilst at Chappel & Wakes Colne the East Anglian Railway Museum has a large selection of rolling stock. This includes an ex-GER coach which the author helped to rescue from Felixstowe!

Right: Haverhill North station pictured from the train on 7 April 1964. Note the blank space on the name board which once informed of the need to change for the Colne Valley line. *Author*

Below: The same view in August 1994. The site remains undeveloped and heavily overgrown. *Author*

Table 26 CHAPPEL AND WAKES COLNE, HALSTEAD and HAVERHILL

Miles		Week Days am		am		pm	pm Z Except Saturdays	pm N Saturdays only						Sundays am		pm F				
	25 London (L'pool St) dep	6 54	..	1036	..	2636	4 56	4 56	..	..	..	..	..	8 15	..	4 45	..	..	..	..
—	**Chappel & Wakes C.** dep	9 14	..	12■9	..	4 45	6 35	6 40	..	..	..	..	..	10 44	..	6 35	..	..	..	..
2	White Colne	9 19	..	1214	..	4 50	6 40	6 45	..	..	..	..	..	10 49	..	6 40	..	..	..	..
3½	Earls Colne	9 23	..	1218	..	4 55	6 45	6 49	..	..	..	..	..	10 54	..	6 44	..	..	..	..
6	**Halstead**	9 31	..	1225	..	5 4	6 58	7 2	..	..	..	..	..	11 3	..	6 51	..	..	..	..
9½	Sible and Castle Hedingham	9 46	..	1232	..	5 12	7 6	7 9	..	..	..	..	..	11 11	..	6 58	..	..	..	..
12	Yeldham	9 52	..	1238	..	5 18	7 13	7 15	..	..	..	..	..	11 18	..	7 4	..	..	..	..
15¾	Birdbrook	10 0	..	1246	..	5 26	7 22	7 23	..	..	..	..	..	11 28	..	7 12	..	..	..	..
19½	**Haverhill** arr	10 8	..	1254	..	5 34	7B31	7B31	..	..	..	..	..	11B36	..	7B20	..	..	..	..
74½	**25 London** (L'pool St) arr	1239	..	4 52	..	8 40	11c23	9 53	..	..	..	..	..	4 11	..	9t59	..	..	..	..

Miles		Week Days am			am			pm			pm				Sundays am U		pm					
	25 London (L'pool St) dep	4 24	..	..	5 54	..	..	12n24	..	..	3 24	..	..	..	..	..	2 24	..	..	..	..	..
—	**Haverhill** dep	7B11	..	..	9 22	..	..	2 20	..	..	6 5	..	..	..	8B41	..	4B43	..	..	..	..	..
3¾	Birdbrook	7 20	..	..	9 31	..	..	2 29	..	..	6 15	..	..	..	8 51	..	4 52	..	..	..	..	..
7½	Yeldham	7 28	..	..	9 39	..	..	2 37	..	..	6 23	..	..	..	9 0	..	5 2	..	..	..	..	..
10	Sible and Castle Hedingham	7 35	..	..	9 52	..	..	2 44	..	..	6 30	..	..	..	9 7	..	5 9	..	..	..	..	..
13½	**Halstead**	7 46	..	..	10 0	..	..	2 52	..	..	6Y50	..	..	..	9 16	..	5 16	..	..	..	..	..
16	Earls Colne	7 53	..	..	10 6	..	..	2 58	..	..	7Y 3	..	..	..	9 22	..	5 22	..	..	..	..	..
17½	White Colne	7 58	..	..	1011	..	..	3 3	..	..	7Y 8	..	..	..	9 27	..	5 27	..	..	..	..	..
19¾	**Chappel & Wakes C.** arr	8 2	..	..	1015	..	..	3 7	..	..	7Y12	..	..	..	9 31	..	5 31	..	..	..	..	..
69¾	**25 London** (L'pool St) arr	9 57	..	..	1152	..	..	4P34	..	..	9 3	..	..	..	11K15	..	7 20	..	..	..	..	..

B Through Train to or from Cambridge (Table 25)
c From 11th July to 2nd September inclusive arr 9 53 pm
F Through Train from Walton-on-Naze dep 5 25 pm and Clacton-on-Sea dep 5 33 pm (Tables 27, 5 and 25)
6 On Mondays to Fridays until 24th June and from 12th September dep Liverpool Street 2 10 pm
■ On Saturdays until 3rd September inclusive dep Chappel & Wakes Colne 12 5 pm
K On 19th and 26th June arr Liverpool Street 11 35 am
N Through Train from Clacton-on-Sea dep 5 30 pm to Cambridge (Tables 27, 5 and 25)
n Dep 12 10 pm on Saturdays
P Arr 4 41 pm on Saturdays and 4 21 pm on Fridays 1st July to 9th September inclusive
t Arr 10 42 pm until 3rd July and on 11th and 18th September
U Through Train to Clacton-on-Sea arr 10 33 am and Walton-on-Naze arr 10 43 am (Tables 5 and 27)
Y Arrives 6 36 pm
Y Runs 4 mins. later on Saturdays
Z Through Train (27th June to 9th Sept. inclusive) from Walton-on-Naze dep 5 16 pm and Clacton-on-Sea dep 5 22 pm (Tables 27, 5 and 25)

Bottom left: To school by train with plenty of staff to look after you; Linton station on 7 April 1964 taken from the train. The station buildings still remain, in private use, in 1994.
Author

Bottom right: An ex-GER hand lamp dated 1923 and formerly from Haverhill North signalbox.
Author

The station at Clare has been turned into a country park, complete with a short length of track and goods shed containing a freight wagon. A number of other stations on the line, with their distinctive design remain, such as at Long Melford, Linton and Bartlow. Nothing remains of the original station at Sudbury, although an overbridge to the north of the station, which was replaced just before the line closed, does remain.

Both stations at Haverhill have been demolished, but in 1994 the derelict site of the former GER station still lingered on. Yet the Sturmer Arch, a fine and wide, listed red brick bridge, provides a vivid reminder of Haverhill's former railway connections when approaching the town from the southwest.

⑥ Making tracks to Maldon

Maldon was once the second largest settlement in Essex. Although the riverside town had iron industries it became equally a popular resort. It was also an important port on the River Blackwater and remains noted both for its Thames barges and for its production of sea salt — this dry part of the country provides little fresh water to dilute the brine of the sea. The town was first linked to Witham by a six-mile-long branch. This ran along the Blackwater Valley to the port area of Maldon and opened firstly to freight in August 1848 and to passengers in October of the same year.

The Maldon, Witham & Braintree Railway, which ran between those towns, and later westward via Rayne to Bishop's Stortford, was soon taken over by the Eastern Counties Railway. As if to reflect the architectural splendour of Maldon a very fine terminus was erected by the ECR in a colonial Jacobean style in the town. In reality the fact that the Chairman of the ECR aspired to stand as parliamentary candidate for Maldon may have had more to do with the money and time lavished on the building.

A second link from Maldon was opened in October 1889 and ran south some 8¾ miles to join with the line to Burnham-on-Crouch at Woodham Ferrers. This link enabled, by the use of new spurs at Witham, Maldon and Wickford, through passenger services to be provided between Colchester and Southend. However, the through service was not a success and

Below: Rayne station was on one of the routes that ran to Witham and on to Maldon. Of typical GER design in the Essex area the station was being extensively restored for use as an information centre and accommodation for the warden of the Flitch Way in the summer of 1994 when this view was taken. *Author*

Left: The original enamel GER name board at Rayne, taken on 12 September 1959.
R. F. Roberts

Below: One of the original oil lamps from Rayne discovered in an antique shop in Tunbridge Wells in July 1989! Unfortunately the lamp had been sold and the prospective owner intended to remove the Rayne name replacing it with his house number.
Author

ran on Saturdays only for about five years. This new line, was forced to cross the Chelmer and Blackwater Navigation canal and River Blackwater at Maldon on substantial bridges before running into a short tunnel to reach a second station in the town. This was built in less elaborate style and was called Maldon West.

Maldon and the adjoining settlement of Heybridge did not expand as rapidly as some settlements with the coming of the railway, as failure to improve the harbour resulted in only relatively small boats being able to use the port. Maldon West closed as a World War 1 economy measure between 1916 and 1919 and other economies were made on the link to Woodham

Below: BTH Type 1 No D8220 running round its train of three coaches at Maldon East station on 6 August 1960.
F. Church

Above: The impressive Jacobean and colonial style exterior of Maldon East station on 2 May 1964. *L. Sandler*

Right: A similar view of Maldon East station taken in August 1994. While still remaining, the building was unoccupied at this time and in a deteriorating state. *Author*

Below: An ex-GER seat displaying the station's full name of 'Maldon East and Heybridge' preserved at Mangapps Farm Museum in the summer of 1994. *Author*

Ferrers. Attempts were also made to increase revenue by opening halts at Baron's Lane in July 1922 and at Stow St Mary in September 1928. Alas, all these efforts were in vain and the Maldon-Woodham Ferrers line closed to passengers in September 1939 and to freight in April 1953, although an intermittent freight link continued between Maldon East and Maldon West until January 1959. Once the girder bridge across the River Blackwater on this section had been removed, daredevil Eddy Kidd made a successful crossing of the gap left by the bridge on his motorbike!

Diesel trains were introduced on the remaining route to Witham and passenger numbers, particularly commuters to London, were increasing. There was, therefore, considerable anger when it was declared

that in spite of this the line required some capital expenditure and would be closed. In a strange twist of fate the local MP at the time actually supported the Beeching Report and made little effort to save the line. The last passenger train left in September 1964 with the Mayor and Mayoress of Maldon on board, to a mass of detonators and to protest. Freight trains ran until April 1966.

Today the link line between Maldon East and Maldon West stations has been turned into a road and the steep gradient on this former railway route from the port is apparent when driving along the road, although the short tunnel that was provided on this link is no longer in use. Maldon West is in use as an industrial estate. On the route to Witham a wooden trestle bridge remains near Wickham Bishops, as does the beautiful Maldon East station, although in 1994 this was in a derelict and unused state. The Witham-Braintree line remains open.

Left: One of the makeshift station lamps at Wickham Bishops platform, just two weeks before the final passenger service, on 23 August 1964. *G. R. Mortimer*

Below: The rustic Wickham Bishops station on the Maldon-Witham section with a train headed by a Class J15 0-6-0 departing in the early 1950s. *D. Lawrence*

Left: A view looking to Maldon West station from the tunnel on this section of line.
Hugh Davies

Below: The derelict Maldon West station with the bleak looking booking office perched above the short tunnel on this section of line that ran up from Maldon East. This view of dereliction was taken on 3 March 1957.
Hugh Davies

Left: A road overbridge at Cold Norton on the former line between Maldon West and Woodham Ferrers on 3 March 1957. *Hugh Davies*

7 A sea interlude: The lost Master

Harwich has a 1½-mile length of line which closed in March 1883 when the new Parkeston Quay loop was opened. It also has much of railway interest and has been heavily promoted as a port over the years. This chapter, by way of an interlude, is somewhat unrelated to the lost lines at Harwich, but refers to the early loss of a railway steamship and in particular its brave Master.

The former Great Eastern Hotel at Harwich faced the North Sea and towards Europe. Opened in 1865 and closed by 1923 the tranquillity today can belie the fact that in two World Wars the narrow seas in this area were a very hazardous place to be. During World War 1 the hotel was used as an army hospital and it was during this time that this story of the valour of a railway employee, Capt Fryatt, is set.

The steamship *Brussels* operated on the Harwich-Antwerp service, but had been taken over by the Admiralty in World War 1 and was, therefore, a prime target for German U-boats. On 22 June 1916 her Master, Capt Fryatt, was attacked by such a submarine, the U33, in the North Sea. Although defenceless, Capt Fryatt attempted to destroy the submarine by ramming it. He failed in this valiant attempt and was taken as a prisoner-of-war to Bruges. Then, contrary to the Geneva Convention, he was summarily shot for his action. This harsh act outraged the British public and resulted in many a shell being aimed at the Germans with 'for Captain Fryatt' painted upon it.

Such was the feeling of wrongdoing roused by the execution of this intrepid man that after World War 1 Capt Fryatt's body was exhumed and brought back to England. No effort was spared by the Great Eastern Railway in paying tribute to its Captain. On 8 July 1919 a service was held at St Paul's Cathedral with a programme of music by the orchestra of the GER Musical Society. Fryatt's body was then taken to Liverpool Street where a special funeral train hauled by 'Claud Hamilton' class 4-4-0 No 1849 and decorated in black and purple, with a huge wreath in front,

left from platform 9 to the sound of massed bands. Thousands awaited the train's arrival at Dovercourt, Fryatt's final resting place.

Today his grave at Dovercourt remains the most prominent in the churchyard and contains the following inscription that clearly shows the indignation at his execution:

> 'In memory of Captain Charles Algernon Fryatt – Master of the Great Eastern Railway steamship 'Brussels' – Illegally executed by the Germans at Bruges on 27 July 1916 – Erected by the Company as an expression of their admiration of his gallantry.'

A road, the local sea scouts and a public house at Parkeston Quay are all named after Capt Fryatt. Furthermore a memorial to him at

Liverpool Street station states:

> *'From the neutral admirers of his brave conduct and heroic death.'*

The marble and bronze plaque takes pride of place in the new refurbished station.

To conclude this story, after the incident the ship *Brussels* was captured by the Germans and stationed at Zeebrugge. However, a daring raid sunk this boat in the harbour entrance. The boat was salvaged after World War 1 and ran in railway service until 1929.

Opposite top: A nationalistic brochure provided to highlight the death of Captain Fryatt. *Courtesy of Imperial War Museum*

Opposite bottom: The former Great Eastern Hotel at Harwich pictured in August 1994. The hotel, designed by Thomas Allom and long since closed, was used as offices by the local council between 1951 and 1983. *Author*

Above left: The substantial headstone for Captain Fryatt in the churchyard at Dovercourt in July 1984. *Author*

Above right: Part of the bronze and marble memorial to Captain Fryatt at Liverpool Street station photographed here in September 1994. *Author*

Right: On a rather happier note the 'Captain Fryatt' public house at Parkeston Quay photographed in August 1994. *Author*

⑧ The line that refused to die

In May 1877 the Felixstowe Railway & Dock Co opened a branch from Westerfield, on the East Suffolk line, some 14³/₄ miles to Felixstowe Pier at the mouth of the River Orwell. The branch is not a lost line. Although proposed for closure in the Beeching Report, against all the odds Felixstowe remains connected by passenger trains to Ipswich. However, the line's survival owes very much to the development of the port of Felixstowe and the considerable freight generated by this east coast port.

There have been some closures at Felixstowe itself. The Pier station closed in July 1951 and today the site is lost within the port development. Beach station was the next to go, although the wooden buildings and track to the docks remain. Beach station, which was once the main one for the town, was exceptionally well used on summer weekends, but this could not sustain all-year retention and it was closed in September 1967. Felixstowe Town station, a newer terminus, designed by W. N. Ashbee and opened in 1898, was built to serve the Edwardian extension of Felixstowe. The station remains open, albeit cut back to a single platform, whilst the bulk of the terminus is now used for retail purposes.

Fine as the town station and former station hotel opposite are, the finest building in the town, and perhaps on the east coast itself, is the former Felix Hotel. The hotel takes its name from Felix, a monk invited over to East Anglia in the seventh century and who became the first bishop of East Anglia. This substantial building was both designed and built principally by The Hon Douglas Tollemache. The hotel was opened on 12 May 1903.

The GER already had modest hotels in Harwich, Parkeston Quay and Hunstanton. The Felix Hotel was in a different class, but was taken over by the Great Eastern Railway in 1920. Three years later it came under the ownership of the LNER, who after closure for refurbishment, repairs and the addition of some bedrooms, reopened the hotel in March 1925 to much

Below: Felixstowe Town station after World War 1 with a GER 'Claud Hamilton' Class 4-4-0 No 1791 standing resplendent at the terminus awaiting departure. *Locomotive Publishing Co*

Above: A similar view of Felixstowe Town platform taken in August 1994; trains still use the very far end of this platform, but the station itself has been turned into retail uses and a car park. *Author*

Below: Felixstowe Beach signalbox looking towards Felixstowe Town shortly before closure of the station in 1967. Note the gas-lit platform. *Author*

acclaim and publicity as one of the LNER's leading luxury hotels. It became popular with the very rich and was indeed a very splendid hotel. Built on a vast scale in Jacobean style and perched on cliffs with commanding views of the North Sea, the hotel boasted extensive facilities, including 21 tennis courts and had its own cliff gardens leading down to the beach.

Although Felixstowe is unique in facing south on the east coast, and the hotel also faced south, the east coast can suffer from indifferent weather and the bracing east wind — the huge conservatory and various arbour and wind breaks in the hotel gardens are testament to this. This and a general change in holiday travel patterns after World War 2 led to its decline. The hotel was sold in the early 1950s by British Railways to Fisons who turned it into offices. It was eventually sold on and converted into a residential development, but without damage to the integrity of the building.

The many tennis courts once provided for the hotel today form the basis of the Felixstowe Tennis Club, whilst the hotel's cliff gardens are now available to the public. Trains still run to Felixstowe, a line that

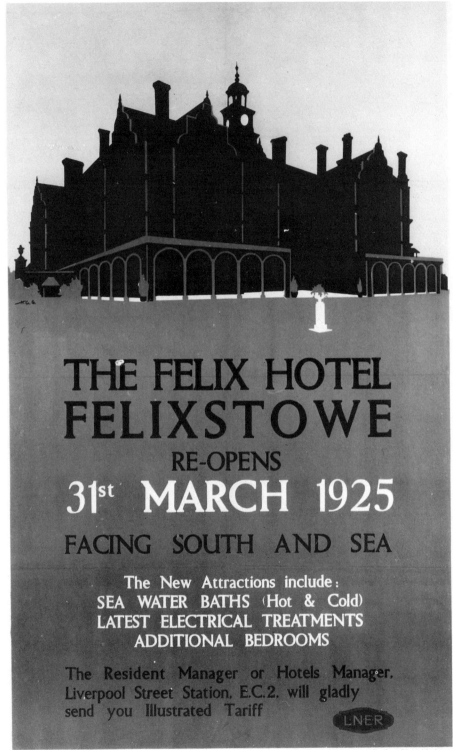

FELIXSTOWE
IT'S QUICKER BY RAIL

FREE ILLUSTRATED GUIDE FROM INFORMATION BUREAU, FELIXSTOWE OR ANY L·N·E·R INQUIRY OFFICE

has refused to die. Indeed uniquely most of the for-mer railway structures associated with the town remain and the direct spur to the docks, closed in 1898, has reopened.

Left: An LNER poster reporting the reopening of the Felix Hotel after extension and improve-ments, including cold water baths! *Courtesy NRM*

Above: The attractive cliff-top location of the Felix Hotel is cap-tured in this artist's illustration by Frank Newbould. The hotel stood in 16 acres of ground. *Courtesy NRM*

Right: The former Felix Hotel has been converted into residential accommodation without damage to the integrity of the building, or its setting, as this view taken in August 1994 shows. *Author*

⑨ Freight-only ports

The Woodbridge Tramway

The attractive town of Woodbridge is situated on raised ground at the head of the tidal section of the River Deben. The river is navigable inland basically as far as Woodbridge and Melton and prior to the advent of the railway provided a means of transporting freight to the area. It was between these two settlements, on reclaimed land between the river and higher land, that the East Suffolk line was built. This section was followed for much of its length by a horse-drawn tramway. The freight-only tramway ran

Above: The Woodbridge Tramway can be seen to the right of the main line in this picture which was taken in the early 1960s from the footbridge at Woodbridge station. *Author*

Left: A similar view taken in 1994, over 30 years later, shows one of the few sections of the tramway route that can still be clearly traced. *Author*

Opposite top left: The vandalised interior of Melton signalbox prior to its total demolition. As a schoolboy the author spent many a Saturday afternoon in this box which was once one of the best kept along the line. *Author*

from sidings on the river side of Woodbridge station towards Melton. Limekiln Quay was served by a separate siding, and a wagon turntable also served a waterside section of tramway along Sun Wharf.

Freight, such as agricultural produce, timber and coal, was interchanged on the quaysides and at Gladwell's merchant's depot to and from the tramway. Traffic could be heavy enough on occasions to necessitate double heading, or perhaps more accurately 'horsing' of trains, Tinker and Charlie being two horses used at Woodbridge for several years. Ash was tipped over the sleepers to give the horses a surer footing and as such the line was justifiably called a tramway. Inevitably such trade declined, the river became unnavigable for many commercial craft and in the early 1960s the tramway was seldom used. All freight workings ended at Woodbridge in July 1966.

There was no extensive signalling here and the tramway operated as a long siding, but at

Woodbridge and for that matter at Melton, the signal boxes were of particular interest. The one at Woodbridge was repainted shortly before being demolished in 1974, whilst at Melton the box lasted for many years longer before it was demolished, although it never had the benefit of a repaint! Indeed there was scepticism that expenses such as repainting signalboxes prior to their demolition were all designed to make the finances of the East Suffolk line look even shakier than perhaps they really were. Whilst the East Suffolk line remains in use, almost all evidence of the tramway has gone.

Snape Maltings

The salt marshes surrounding Snape give the vast and rambling maltings a particular attraction. A short, just over one-mile freight line operated from Snape Junction, north of Campsey Ash, to Snape and the maltings. The line was opened in June 1859 and it is

clear from the design of the station house at Snape that it was intended for possible future passenger use as the building would have required little adaptation to make it into a passenger terminus.

The maltings were sited some way from the small village of Snape itself and it was decided that traffic would not justify the expense of building a junction station on the main line to introduce passenger trains. Nevertheless the branch was kept busy with freight associated with the maltings. At its peak many thousands of tons of barley and malt were conveyed over the line annually, whilst coal, coke and interchange merchandise with the River Alde were also sources of income to the branch. Locomotives were not allowed into the maltings themselves as there were no run round facilities and wagons were towed across the road, firstly by horses, but in later days by a tractor adapted to push the wagons. Such was the scale of the operation that an internal narrow gauge line at one time linked the malt store to the quay.

Although general freight used the line and for a time after World War 2 rubble from war-damaged London was dumped at Snape Bridge, the fortunes of the branch were inextricably linked to the maltings. Indeed the line was closed for a short time during World War 1 during a barley shortage, but final

Above right: A view of the sidings at the Woodbridge station end of the tramway being dismantled in the 1960s. *Author*

Centre: Woodbridge signalbox looking absolutely immaculate after an expensive restoration and repainting. Shortly after this was completed the box was taken out of use and demolished! *Author*

Right: This view of Woodbridge Quay taken on 20 May 1958 shows the tramway line visible in front of the main line crossing gates. *Author's Collection*

closure did not come until March 1960. After a time of inactivity the maltings became world famous as home for the Aldeburgh Festival and music of Benjamin Britten. The station house remains at Snape and an old covered wagon, whilst the branch can still be traced for part of its route.

Blackshore Quay

The 3ft gauge Southwold Railway never formed any part of Eastern Region, having closed as early as 1929. It was unique in that it was the only passenger-carrying narrow gauge railway in the area and there has always been a nostalgic hankering for its return. Where it reached the coast at Blythburgh it passed through a marvellous coastal area known as The Heronry, before crossing the River Blyth and running through a cutting on the edge of Southwold Common to reach Southwold itself.

As a way of relieving the growing congestion at Lowestoft harbour, consideration was given to improving Southwold harbour. In 1914 a one-mile spur was run down from a point west of the Southwold terminus to the north side of the River Blyth, with a junction to Blackshore Quay a little up stream, but also on the Blyth. The port at Southwold was not a massive affair, being essentially concrete piers to the north and south at the mouth of the river, together with a jetty. At first much of the freight was associated with defences for World War 1. Indeed in 1917 large numbers of Dutch and Belgian nationals were repatriated from the port, although only their baggage was conveyed by train. In later years fishing smacks and barges could be seen, but the port never developed substantial commercial traffic and the railway connection closed, together with the entire Southwold Railway, in April 1929.

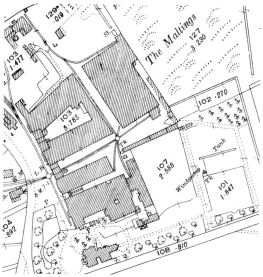

Even in the 1960s it was possible to find relics of Southwold Railway, including the unique clips that secured the rails and even the odd length of rail. A footbridge that crossed the railway at Southwold Common, that was itself made of old rails, but had become unsafe, was cut down in the early 1960s. The main station building at Southwold also survived long after closure, but was eventually demolished to give way to a police and fire station, although one of the three horse chestnut trees that were planted along the platform still survived in 1994. A short section of the railway line at Blackshore Quay, including the solid wood buffer stop which looks remarkably like the nearby groynes, also survives. It is remarkable that such remains still exist so long after closure of the line.

Top left: A Southwold Railway flat-bottomed track clip found near Blackwater Quay in the 1960s. *R.Trill*

Top right: An abandoned freight wagon at Snape in August 1994. *Author*

Below: Narrow gauge tracks lead down to Blackwater Quay from the main line. *M. Bristow Collection*

Lowestoft sleeper depot

There was a time when almost all sleepers were made of wood and many of those in the ER, some still existing, would have been made at the Lowestoft sleeper depot. The GER and later the LNER used Lowestoft to import timber for sleepers and a 1,000ft quay and narrow gauge railway were provided at one time. At

the depot timber was cut to the required sizes and then hundreds of slits were punched in the wood before the resulting sleepers were creosoted to preserve them. An extract from the diary explains a birthday treat for myself:

Saturday, 9 May 1964: Today I went round Lowestoft sleeper depot. They were making the last sleepers and all the men I met were going to get the sack. Saw Sentinel engines No 7 and No 40. No 7 was due to be scrapped next Monday. It was also 40's last day of working and I rode on the engine. It filled with steam and was a very rough, slow ride. The engine was fuelled by wood, which were bits of old sleepers.

No 40 was in fact a Class Y3 0-4-0, a geared locomotive with a short wheelbase made by Sentinel. I can recall even today the pleasantness and cheerfulness of staff at this depot in spite of the fact that it was about to close and they were about to lose their jobs.

Above: Quayside tracks at Southwold.
M. Bristow Collection

Below left: Sentinel locomotive, Class Y3, BR No (6)8177 at Lowestoft Yard on 21 June 1951. Clearly these machines could run on wood as well as coal, but the riding qualities in the cab in hot weather and on rough track were none too pleasant. *E. M. Patterson*

Below right: A short length of Southwold Railway track remains at Blackwater Quay on the River Blyth, as this photograph taken September 1994 shows. The museum at Southwold and the East Anglia Transport Museum near Lowestoft both contain relics of the line. *Author*

10 A branch to nowhere

The heart of Suffolk has changed little over the years. The rolling hills and winding lanes provide an attractive area, but were not the most lucrative of areas for railways. The 'Middy', as the Mid-Suffolk Light Railway was known, was a light railway running from its own terminus at Haughley (East) some 21 miles to Cratfield sidings. It was, as the name implies, a lightly constructed railway that had just one overbridge and three road underbridges, but over a hundred road or occupation crossings on its route.

The line opened for freight traffic as far as Laxfield in September 1904 and this service had been extended to Cratfield by 1906. There were delays in upgrading the route for passenger traffic, but the first passenger train ran to Laxfield by September 1908. The original intent was to extend the line some six miles or so to Halesworth, on the East Suffolk Line,

and then to convert the Southwold Railway to standard gauge; creating a through route from the Midlands to the North Sea at Southwold. A second 13½-mile link was also intended to run south through Debenham to join the East Suffolk line at Westerfield, but in fact ran only 2¼ miles from Kenton Junction to the banks of the River Deben, just short of the proposed station at Debenham.

Had all the planned routes been constructed the lines might have stood more chance of success. As it was, decline set in early. In February 1912 the freight-only Cratfield section closed and trains ran just beyond Laxfield to Laxfield Mills. Cattle docks, which had been provided at most stations, became increasingly less used as agriculture in the area turned from cattle to corn; this again reduced revenue on the line. During World War 1 track was lifted on the section

Left: A rather rickety Laxfield shed, at the end of the line, photographed on 5 July 1936 with a Class J65 0-6-0T No 7253 posing outside. *H. C. Casserley*

Below: Class J15 0-6-0 No 65447 photographed at Laxfield with the 1.45pm to Haughley. This view of rural tranquillity was taken at 1.33pm on 5 July 1952. *G. R. Mortimer*

from Kenton to near Debenham and any chance of the original plans to reach the East Suffolk line was ended, both by lack of capital and by objection from the GER. Thus it was the line ended up as a rural spur terminating in fields near Laxfield.

Services were slow and in its unfinished state the line missed some of the main population and commercial centres in a sparsely populated area and as such always remained a secondary backwater in financial trouble. Indeed the LNER was reluctant to take over the line and the first act when the ER took over was to close the route. Final trains ran in July 1952 when special arrangements had to be made to cope with the crowds wishing to say goodbye to the 'Middy'.

Above: Haughley Junction station pictured with the 10.22am Ipswich-Bury St Edmunds train standing on the down main line and with a mixed freight and passenger train for Laxfield in the bay platform on 23 July 1952, a few days prior to closure. The London suburban coaches had replaced six-wheeled stock on the line the previous year. R. E. Vincent

Left: The former Mid-Suffolk Light Railway seen on the final day of services. This view is of the 3.55pm Saturdays only service from Haughley to Laxfield near Mendlesham. This was the last scheduled run, but was followed by a special return. Class J15 No 65447 with the driver J. Skinner, fireman J. A. Law and R. H. N. Hardy, then locomotive shedmaster at Ipswich, on the footplate hauls a packed and delayed train on 26 July 1952. The service was running about 45min late. G. R. Mortimer

Above: The last train of all — Haughley station seen after the arrival of the closing special from Laxfield. The train was hauled by Class J15 No 65447 with driver Skinner on the footplate. Some of the onlookers' attention was diverted by a down 'Britannia'-powered express when this view was taken at 7.30pm on 26 July 1952. *G. R. Mortimer*

Below The ex-GER Haughley Junction station was a substantial affair and remained open after the closure of the former Mid Suffolk Light Railway line, as this view taken later in 1953 shows. *Real Photographs Co*

Being lightly constructed, even in the early 1960s much of the route had been reclaimed for agriculture or was heavily overgrown and it was impossible to travel very far on foot from Haughley along the old line. A section of overgrown embankment remains north of Debenham and it looked as if the 'Middy'

would be just a memory, but this was not to be so.

Closure was not to be the end of the story as preservationists now hold out hopes of an afterlife. A surprising amount remains. One of the distinctive lettered name boards from Kenton is preserved at the National Railway Museum. Both Horham and

Right: One of the few substantial remaining earthworks of the old Mid Suffolk Light Railway can still be found to the north of Debenham where an arched brick bridge once crossed the road. This substantially overgrown section of the line was abandoned as far back as World War 1. Author

Below right: Although one of the original locally-made Mid Suffolk name boards is preserved at the NRM at York, a replica sign has been made for Brockford station and is shown here in August 1994. Author

Below: Another view of the several well preserved former Mid Suffolk Light Railway buildings at Brockford station taken in August 1994. Author

Laxfield station buildings survived and have been preserved at the Mangapps Farm Railway Museum in Essex. The remains of the old cattle dock at Brockford station have been restored and extended to the standard 130ft-long Mid-Suffolk station platform. Track has been relaid and rolling stock with associations to the line assembled. Three former Mid Suffolk station buildings have also been preserved on the site. The original corrugated iron booking office/staff room from Brockford station was found at nearby Old Newton and a similar building, formerly at Wilby, was also located and moved to Brockford. The Wilby building still retained its original furniture. The largest of the three buildings discovered was the original station building from Mendlesham, which was also moved to Brockford. A level crossing has been created at the station and the eventual intention is to run a stretch of the line towards Aspall.

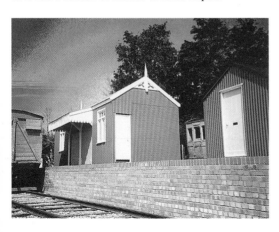

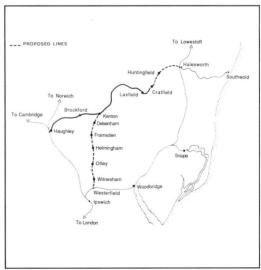

11 The last train from Aldeburgh

The line from Saxmundham to Aldeburgh was originally planned to run east only as far as Leiston to serve Richard Garrett's engineering works, but was extended the full 8¼ miles to Aldeburgh and opened in April 1860. Aldeburgh in the 17th century was an important port and even on the opening of the branch produced a considerable amount of fish freight. However, the ever changing Suffolk coast caused the development of shingle banks on the River Alde and the general decline of Aldeburgh as a port.

It was hoped that the decline in the port would be arrested by proposals for a new port, but the plans met with objection and freight on the line continued to decline. On the other hand tourism on the line grew, particularly in the peak summer months and in July 1914 a halt, utilising old railway carriages, was opened to the north of Aldeburgh at Thorpeness. Excursions were run to Aldeburgh and on occasions the luxury Pullman train, the *Eastern Belle*, included the branch as one of its destinations.

In June 1956 DMUs took over operation of the branch and a number of through services operated to

Left: Internally Leiston signalbox was very well kept. This view shows a DMU leaving Leiston for Aldeburgh on 28 June 1961. S. Creer

Below: An Ipswich-Aldeburgh special excursion for the Aldeburgh regatta in August 1955 sees 'J15' No 65467 storming away after having had to stop at the foot of the bank to take the staff for the first section of the Aldeburgh branch. Dr Ian C. Allen

Right: A train from Saxmundham hauled by ex-GER 2-4-2T No 67239 arrives at Aldeburgh at 1.45pm on 25 June 1951. E. M. Patterson

Below right: A view showing the rather dark overall train shed at Aldeburgh station in 1952. Note the window boxes at the front of the station. Real Photographs Co

Below: Leiston station pictured with the 5.6pm Aldeburgh-Saxmundham train leaving for Saxmundham. Ignore the indicator blind! The track to the right of the view formed part of the once extensive transfer sidings for Richard Garrett's Engineering Works. This view on 6 September 1966 was taken during the last week of passenger services. G. R. Mortimer

Ipswich. In spite of this, the line saw a period of decline and from November 1959 freight no longer used the Aldeburgh terminal. However, the station gardens at Aldeburgh remained one of the delights of the whole region. In fact since the best kept garden competition began in 1923 Mr Botterill, the porter, ticket collector and booking clerk, won for Aldeburgh no less than 36 certificates including 18 specials. In no year did Aldeburgh fail to gain an award and if you saw the garden, with its immaculate lawn and flowers, you soon realised why.

The resplendent gardens were to the front of the station, in contrast to the platform which was covered by an overall roof which was dark and forbidding.

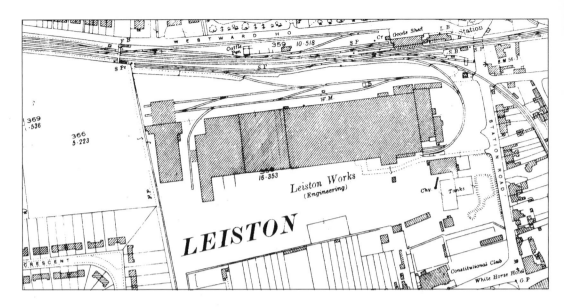

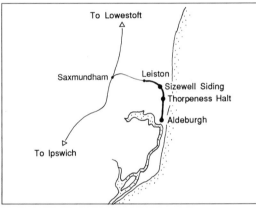

This was removed and the signalbox taken out of use
before this section of the line closed. The station platforms remained gas lit until the end and the branch
closed in September 1966.

An extract from the diary recalls the last passenger train on the Aldeburgh branch:

*Saturday, 10 September 1966: Went to Aldeburgh
on the last train. The train was packed, as was the
platform at Saxmundham and there was a mad rush
to get on. The train left totally full and some
passengers wore black ties. Leiston station was also
packed with people and all along the route people
came out of their houses to see the last train.
Thorpeness station was covered with flags.
Aldeburgh station was also packed and everyone was
taking hundreds of photographs. As the train left,
detonators rang out over the town, everybody waved
en route. We waited for ages at Thorpeness where a
flag said 'Give us back our trains'. I thought they*

Above: The same view taken in 1980. Much of the station site had been converted to residential use. The beautiful gardens have gone, but the Scots pine trees remain. Author

Right: Handbill for the Aldeburgh branch

would never be able to unpadlock the gates. As we finally went on to Leiston, those living by the line lit flares and bonfires; detonators went off at each crossing. We left Leiston with the hooter going like mad, everybody was waving furiously, arrived at Saxmundham Junction to more detonators, then even more at Saxmundham station, before the train left for Ipswich very late indeed.

Aldeburgh station was subsequently demolished and the site redeveloped for housing. The station gardens are no more, but the Scots pine trees, a feature of many GER stations remain. The branch itself remains open for freight to sidings north of Thorpeness in connection with Sizewell nuclear power station.

GREAT EASTERN

TLM3
Amended Issue from
10th June 1962

SPECIAL
CHEAP DAY TICKETS

ANY DAY   ANY TRAIN

IPSWICH
ALDEBURGH
LOWESTOFT
CENTRAL
YARMOUTH
SOUTH TOWN

AVAILABLE OUTWARD AND RETURN ON DAY OF ISSUE IN EITHER DIRECTION BETWEEN ANY TWO STATIONS SHOWN OVERLEAF

Tickets can be obtained IN ADVANCE at stations and travel agents appointed by British Railways.

Further information will be supplied on application to stations, offices, travel agents appointed by British Railways or to:—

Traffic Manager, Norwich (Thorpe) (Tel. Norwich 20371)
Commercial Officer, Ipswich (Tel. Ipswich 56331)

Children under three years of age, free; three years and under fourteen, half-fares

THIS SUPERSEDES HANDBILL 4094

London: June 1962

Published by British Railways (Eastern Region)   Printed in Great Britain   Modern Press (Nch.) Ltd.

Terminal tales

Eye

The main line from London to Norwich passes many a closed station and junction. One such example is Mellis, between Ipswich and Norwich.

The town of Eye was known to Romans, Saxons and Normans, but in later years had declined and was missed by the main line to Norwich by some three

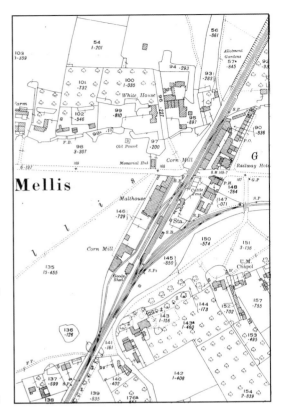

Right: Map of Mellis Junction. Crown Copyright

Below: The old and new meet at Mellis Junction in June 1956. A 'J17' 0-6-0 No 65542 on the Eye branch goods meets the Norwich-Ipswich diesel train on the main line. Dr Ian C. Allen

miles. The Mellis & Eye Railway opened a branch to the town in April 1867, but this did little to revive the town's fortunes. The GER eventually took over and an intermediate halt was provided at Yaxley in December 1922, but the line closed to passengers as far back as February 1931. Freight, mainly agricultural produce and including sugar beet, continued until July 1964. Mellis closed in November 1966, together with most other intermediate stations on the main line from Ipswich to Norwich. Little remains of the branch today, but some of the buildings remain at Eye and parts of the platform at Mellis and a bridge under the A140.

Above: Eye station yard seen in the early 1960s with little rail activity visible. Author's Collection

Below:
Another view of the rambling buildings at Eye station yard pictured in the 1960s. Author's Collection

Yarmouth South Town

Great Yarmouth developed as the port for Norwich, but also developed as a port in its own right. It became a substantial holiday resort and with its famous racecourse the area expanded rapidly. The railways played a great part in this development, there being lines to London via Beccles, Lowestoft, Norwich and to the Midlands via the M&GN line.

Below: The elegant, if somewhat run-down, Yarmouth South Town station frontage caught by the camera in LNER days. Eventually, before final closure, the station became an unstaffed halt. H. C. Casserley

Right: A Metro-Cammell DMU leaves Yarmouth South Town for Halesworth on 11 September 1963. S. Creer

Below: Yarmouth South Town in its declining last years as a DMU waits for departure to Lowestoft. Ian Allan Library

Rationalisation has meant that all lines with the exception of those to Norwich have since been lost.

The main line from Yarmouth South Town to London ran some 12½ miles directly to Beccles over an area of The Broads involving a difficult swing bridge at St Olaves. One of the early rationalisations of the Eastern Region was to close this direct route over the bridge in November 1959. Whilst this was perhaps a little unfortunate, only two people objected. The closure enabled Yarmouth-London services to be diverted over the former Norfolk & Suffolk Joint Railway via Lowestoft.

The change was of benefit to some stations on the joint line, for a time, but did add over six miles to the London-Yarmouth route, which made the later diversion of trains via Norwich more acceptable. Thus it was that in spite of the extra revenue brought to the joint line by the closure of the St Olaves route and the economies in making stations into unstaffed halts, the change was unable to save the well constructed and well-used 10¼-mile line from Lowestoft to the Yarmouth South Town terminus which closed in May 1970. South Town was the finer station in Yarmouth, rather superior to the alternative Yarmouth Vauxhall station. As it happens South Town has since been demolished and after time as a pipeline depot was replaced by a garage selling Vauxhall motor vehicles!

13 Breckland and Broadland byways

Swaffham-Thetford

A curious sense of beauty broods over the Norfolk Breckland. The ancient heaths have seen many a change, including the last of the British great bustards — birds as large as turkeys. Railways are not extinct in the area, but are depleted in their coverage.

The 22¾-mile link from Thetford to Swaffham developed as two separate lines. The Thetford & Watton Railway opened the first section from Roudham Junction, on the main Ely-Norwich line, to Watton for freight in January 1869 and to all traffic by October of that year. In September 1875 the Watton & Swaffham Railway opened a northern 9½-mile extension connecting Watton with Swaffham and making a link line that, by use of a connecting spur north of Thetford Bridge station, enabled trains to be run directly between Bury St Edmunds and Swaffham.

Not surprisingly, the companies found difficulties in raising money to serve this remote and sparsely populated area and the GER took over in 1879. The

Left: A Swaffham-Thetford DMU passes Roudham Junction signalbox and grass-covered platforms in October 1958. Note that the GER lower quadrant signals are about to be replaced by standard BR upper quadrant signals. Hugh Davies

Below: Wretham & Hockham station in September 1994, safely restored as a private dwelling. Author

GER soon ended the through workings from Bury St Edmunds to Swaffham and the Thetford Bridge spur was closed as far back as 1880. Roudham Junction was closed in May 1932, although unadvertised stops were made there and the platforms remained for much longer.

For many years the threat of closure hung over the line which did little to encourage traffic. Nevertheless, in its later years, the line served the important RAF station at Watton and there was still some agricultural freight. Passenger closure came in June 1964 while freight continued until April of the following year. Although always a backwater, stations often built in local flint were both attractive and well kept, some winning a number of prizes. Wretham survives and Swaffham in particular remains as a

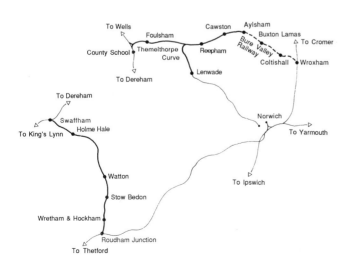

Above: Stow Bedon station signalbox and crossing.
H. C. Casserley

Above left: Stow Bedon station has not survived, as this photograph taken in September 1994 shows. Author

substantial and fine flint-built Jacobean-styled building. Indeed the church in the town contains a beautiful Book of Hours, not I hasten to say the forerunner of the shift system!

Wroxham-County School

The Norfolk Broads, once an arm of the sea, contain about 5,000 acres of waterway, much of this being flooded peat pits, together with miles of river. The area also once contained miles of railway, but a number of lines have been lost. The 23¾-mile line from Wroxham, on the Norwich-Cromer line, running to County School, on the Dereham-Wells-next-the-Sea line, was designed both to compete with the M&GN for east-west traffic in Norfolk and to provide a service to the town of Aylsham which had missed out on earlier railway construction. Although the line did not pass through an area of great physical difficulties, construction was none too rapid. The East Norfolk Railway extended to Aylsham in January 1880 and after being taken over by the GER, reached County School, so named after a nearby school, in May 1882.

Aylsham had flourished principally because of its position on the River Bure and did not develop as expected when the railway reached the town. Furthermore the M&GN also provided a station in the town which reduced the use of the GER line. Thus it was that the GER line remained somewhat of a backwater and although RAF stations brought traffic during World War 2, the line closed to

Above: Watton (Norfolk) station name board taken from the train on 13 June 1963. Note the steps below the name board due to the very low platform at Watton and also the continuing freight activity on the line at this time. Author

Below: The former engine shed and water tower at Watton in 1958, clearly put to good alternative use for agricultural storage. Hugh Davies

Above: The attractive and distinctive Jacobean influenced and flint exterior of Swaffham station taken in March 1962. Real Photographs Co

Below: A similar view of Swaffham taken in September 1994. Although, at first glance, the station appears to have undergone very little alteration, closer examination shows numerous changes, including the loss of chimneys, stone capping, canopy and the thin gable windows. Author

passenger traffic in September 1952 and to all traffic between Foulsham and Reepham.

However, on the closure of the nearby M&GN system a connection from the former GER Aylsham branch was made to the remaining ex-M&GN Melton Constable-Norwich freight line near Themelthorpe and opened in 1960. This allowed freight trains still to reach Norwich City station by a 40-mile route travelling north to Aylsham and then back south via the new curve and Lenwade. Services were later cut back to Lenwade on the M&GN line whilst the section from Foulsham to County School closed for freight in October 1964. Regular freight traffic via the Themelthorpe curve to Lenwade ran until January 1982.

Above: Coltishall station in August 1976, together with other stations on the line, looked as if it could have a bleak future. Coltishall was put up to be let, but was derelict and being vandalised when this view was taken. Author

Left: Decay and demolition was not to be the end. Where buildings remained they have been put to good use and are generally in a respectable condition, as this view of Coltishall station taken in September 1994 shows. Author

Below left: A narrow gauge Bure Valley train passes the site of Buxton Lamas station in September 1994 with a train from Wroxham to Aylsham hauled by the line's diesel-hydraulic locomotive. Author

Right: Swaffham station for Castle Acre — the tourist potential of secondary routes was capitalised on by the LNER as this poster of the Norman west front of Castle Acre Priory shows. Courtesy NRM

CASTLE ACRE PRIORY

CASTLE ACRE
(SWAFFHAM STATION)

IT'S QUICKER BY RAIL

FULL INFORMATION FROM L·N·E·R OFFICES AND AGENCIES

Above: Although the original GER station at Aylsham has been demolished, the location is used today and probably provides the best ever passenger railway facilities on this site. This view looking towards Wroxham is taken from under the overall roof of the new station. Author

Below: A view at County School station taken in September 1994 and looking north towards the former triangular junction for Wroxham at Broom Green. Author

This was not the end of the line. At County School the station has been restored and a railway centre established using a section of the Wells-Dereham branch. At Reepham the station provides a collection of curios and cycles for use on parts of the former GER and M&GN lines now known as Marriott's Way. Finally, the nine-mile section from Wroxham to Aylsham reopened in July 1990 as the 1ft 3in narrow gauge Bure Valley Railway.

14 A royal gateway

Until the coming of the railway Hunstanton was a small coastal village. However, the opening of the 15-mile Lynn & Hunstanton Railway in October 1862 transformed the fortunes of this west facing seaside settlement with its unusual and attractive red and white cliffs and shelving sandy beaches. A pier was

Below: An entrance befitting royalty was provided to the state waiting room at Wolferton station. It was photographed in August 1966. P. Hocquard

Above left: Wolferton station platform, looking towards King's Lynn, photographed in August 1966. P. Hocquard

Above right: A similar platform view at Wolferton station recorded in August 1994. Although the track has gone, little real change is evident. Author

built in 1870, a GER-owned hotel in 1876 and other holiday facilities made the town an ever growing and popular resort.

The route from King's Lynn to Hunstanton was built close to the shores of the Wash without great difficulty. The line passed by Castle Acre and the Sandringham estate. The latter was to provide the branch with notoriety as in 1862 the then Prince of Wales, later to become Edward VII, purchased the Sandringham estate.

The royal link provided the line with prestigious revenue and over the years some of the most famous and powerful people in the world used the line. Indeed, Wolferton station, which was the nearest for Sandringham, was at first improved by the Prince of Wales at his own expense. The rival M&GN also had a station near the royal estate at Hillington and the GER, concerned that they could forfeit royal patronage, improved Wolferton station in the 1890s.

W. N. Ashbee designed a much-improved and elegant mock Tudor-styled station, complete with fine panelling, carving and gold leaf, all of which was to royal approval. Furthermore, to ensure safety and because of increasing traffic, the line from King's Lynn was doubled as far as Wolferton by 1899.

In the years that followed royalty regularly used the line, whilst general passenger trains were run from London and other towns and traffic on the line continued to develop. Even in the 1950s the many caravans in this area added to the line's heavy summer traffic. The royal funeral train of King George VI ran to silent trackside crowds in 1952. The following year the branch was severely hit by the east coast floods of January 1953. Such was the height of sea water that a train on the line had its fire extinguished and the

Above: Wolferton station on the final day of services. The 14.04 Hunstanton-King's Lynn DMU train calls at the station on 3 May 1969. The sign to the right of the train was part of the level crossing modernisation undertaken on this route before its closure. G. R. Mortimer

Left: A similar view of Wolferton station taken in August 1994. Again, fortunately, little significant change has occurred to the Ashbee-designed station structures. Author

Left: Wolferton station signal-box seen from the train on a wet and cold February day in 1969, the final year of services. Author

Below: A similar view taken in August 1994. The signalbox, subsequently resold at auction, remains largely unchanged since closure of the line. Author

branch was unable to reopen until the end of February. Damage caused by the flooding in this part of Norfolk was so severe that the line running from Heacham, some 18¼ miles to Wells-next-the-Sea, which had in fact closed to passengers in 1952, closed completely as a through route as a result of the destruction caused by the floods.

Trains originally ran from the Hunstanton branch

Right: Snettisham signalbox survived the closure and is today preserved in first class condition as this view taken in August 1994 shows. Author

Below: Snettisham station on the final day of service, 3 May 1969, with the 15.00 DMU King's Lynn-Hunstanton service visible. The poor condition of the disused signalbox can be seen in this view. G. R. Mortimer

to many destinations, but the introduction of DMUs in 1958 led to the curtailment of many through services and the start of the decline of the line. The royal trains themselves became less frequent with the royal family completing journeys from London at King's Lynn. Nevertheless, economies were made in modernising road crossings, reducing the remaining double-line section and by the use of conductor guards.

The line was not one of those listed for closure in the Beeching report and by the implementation of

economies it was anticipated that the line would not be closed. Nevertheless, the last royal train used the line in 1966 and in May 1969 the branch closed amidst considerable protest.

Of the many lines to have closed in Norfolk that from Hunstanton to King's Lynn has been the subject of continued calls for reopening. The station at Hunstanton has been demolished, together with the former GER hotel and remains of the pier which was mainly destroyed in a gale in 1968. Today the vast

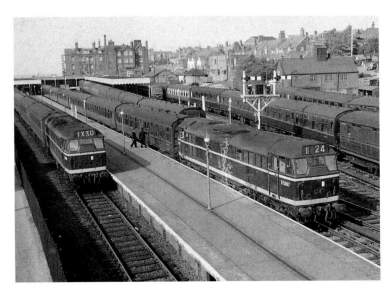

Above: The heyday of Hunstanton station in August 1929. An ex-GER Class JF3 2-4-2T heads the 2.18pm for King's Lynn. A Class D13 4-4-0 awaits with the 2.33pm for Liverpool Street. The station was an absolute hive of activity at this time. Ian Allan Library

Left: Even in the 1960s Hunstanton was very busy during the summer peak. This view of Brush Type 2s Nos D5563 and D5567 shows the station being used to capacity on 27 August 1961. R. J. Smith

Left: This view of the substantial Hunstanton signalbox was also taken in February 1969 and shows the general air of dereliction at the station. Although a number of sidings, operated by ground frames, still remained in anticipation of possible future summer excursion trains, this was not to be and the station never survived into the summer season. Author

Below: In spite of vigorous protests the line did not survive. This view taken in August 1994 shows that the former expansive station at Hunstanton has been given over mainly to a large car park. Author

size of Hunstanton station can be gauged by the shops, car and bus parks that cover the site. Other stations on the line have been more fortunate and most remain in private use. Plans to demolish Wolferton were turned down and today the station acts as a museum containing, in addition to its many royal items, the two wreaths which adorned the last passenger trains to use the line.

The Midland & Great Northern Joint Railway (M&GN) was formed from a number of smaller independent lines by an Act of Parliament in 1893. This was a cross country route linking the East Midlands to the Norfolk coast. It ran from Little Bytham, to the west of Bourne, through Spalding and from Peterborough, via Wisbech, to Sutton Bridge over the rich agricultural fenlands to King's Lynn. Continuing eastward the line ran across Norfolk to Melton Constable, where branches connected to Cromer Beach and Norwich City, whilst the main line continued towards Yarmouth Beach. The M&GN routes once covered a total of over 180 miles.

Although King's Lynn could claim to be the administrative headquarters, certainly in terms of engineering activity Melton Constable was the hub of the system. No fewer than four lines converged on Melton Constable, from Cromer, Yarmouth, Norwich and

King's Lynn. The town possessed its own workshops which made many of the M&GN's locomotives, and the works developed considerable facilities. It became known as 'The Crewe of North Norfolk'. Indeed it had many of the same elements as Crewe, but also boasted a model village of considerable variation, a well respected refreshment room and a private waiting room for the local lord of the manor.

The decline came as a result of rationalisation which allowed the LNER to transfer operations from Melton Constable to other centres and later the ER to transfer traffic to other routes. The main closure came in February 1959 when most former M&GN lines were shut to passenger services. Nevertheless, train services remained from Melton Constable to Sheringham. This line was not to survive the Beeching cuts and all passenger services ended at Melton Constable in April 1964. Even then it was

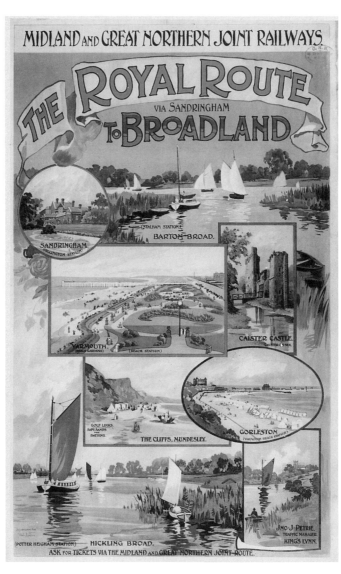

Above: This poster of the 'Royal Route' shows many of the attractions along the M&GN line. It was the M&GN's royal pretensions to the Sandringham Estate and the threat of royalty using its nearby Hillington station that persuaded the GER to improve its Wolferton station. Courtesy NRM

Above: South Lynn station - of interest are the platform edge markings which were introduced as part of the World War 2 blackout measures. The broken line eventually became a continuous one. Also of note is the colour light signal, quite an unusual feature on the former M&GN line. Real Photographs Co

somehow considered that Melton Constable, this former huge hive of activity, would be able to retain some sort of freight service, but unfortunately this expired by the end of the year.

Melton Constable therefore, closed completely and the romantic-sounding town has redeveloped the station and works as an industrial estate. Yet much of the railway flavour remains, including the model village, several railway buildings and the vast triple water tanks on the former works site. Indeed the main industrial estate road is called Marriott Way after the ambidextrous engineer and locomotive superintendent connected with the M&GN system. Moreover, a 5¼-mile section of the line from Melton

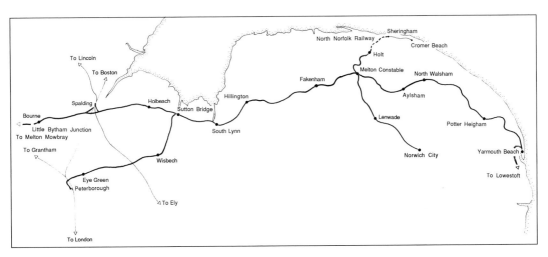

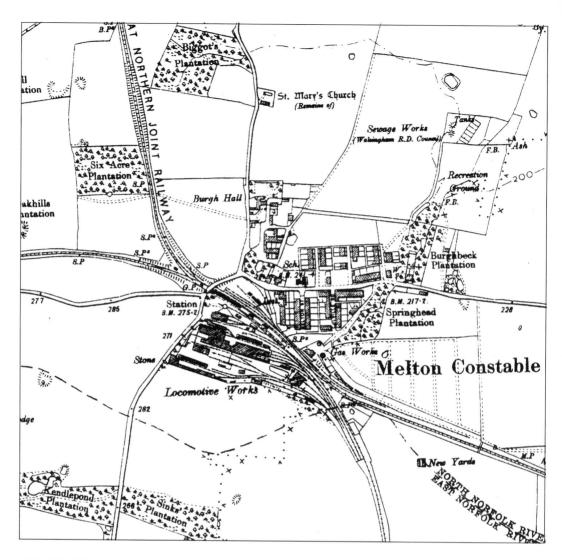

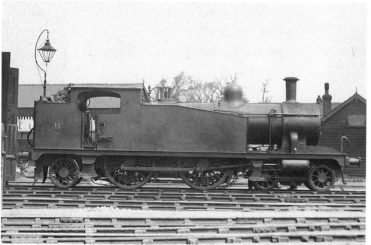

Above: Melton Constable 1907. Crown Copyright

Left: An M&GN 4-4-2T, although recently taken over by the LNER, retaining its old M&GN No 41, stands where it was built in the Melton Constable works complex in May 1937. Real Photographs Co

Left: The aptly named Marriott Way that leads today into the former M&GN works site at Melton Constable. William Marriott uniquely combined his office of Civil Engineer with that of Locomotive Superintendent. Author

Below: The enormous derelict water tank at Melton Constable still remained in 1994 as a monument to the former works site. Each of the many panels that form the vast water tank area are stamped with the M&GN initials. Author

Constable towards Cromer remains in use between Sheringham and Holt operated by the North Norfolk Railway. The line from North Walsham is a footpath called Weavers Way whilst other sections are in use as footpaths or roads.

Above: A view taken in June 1964 looking towards Yarmouth at Potter Heigham Bridge Halt after closure of the line. The single-line bridge over the River Thurne had three 79ft truss spans. Ian Allan Library

Left: The derelict remains of the M&GN station at Aylsham North on 19 June 1965. Note the much smaller scale (but similar design) of water tank to that at Melton Constable. A. Muckley

Above: A section of former
M&GN line has been preserved
between Sheringham and Holt by
the North Norfolk Railway. This
view shows diesel railbus
No E79960 passing Weybourne
outer home somersault signal
while returning from Holt with
the 11.40 service on 27 July
1988. J. Knight

Right: Cromer Beach station
viewed here at the turn of the
century remains open. The overall roof has since been removed
and the goods yard to the left of
this photograph has been turned
into a retail development.
Locomotive Publishing Co

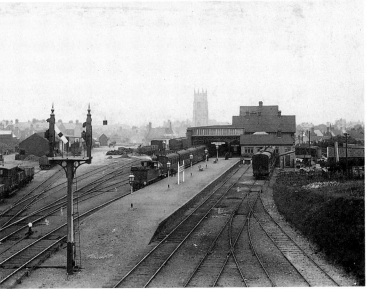

The diary records:

Monday, 6 April 1964: Today we went only as far as Sheringham. Melton Constable was closed on Saturday night. We sat in the train at Sheringham until someone came up to ask where we were going. 'Melton Constable closed last week' he said in a Norfolk accent. We were very disappointed. The local paper reported the fact under the heading 'Ghost train leaves deserted Melton Constable'. We then went to Mundesley-on-Sea where tickets were issued on the train. On return we met a quaint old stationmaster at North Walsham. He said we had time for tea. We only had about 2 minutes before our train came. We saw the disused M&GN North Walsham station.

Above: The North Norfolk Railway, which runs the line from Sheringham to Holt, possesses a number of interesting locomotives including this Class J15 0-6-0 No 7564 seen here standing at Weybourne station, in unlined LNER black livery, just after arriving with its train from Sheringham in September 1981. B. Fisher

Left: Although most of the M&GN line has gone, much has been preserved. This M&GN marker was noted in August 1994 some way from its native territory at the Mangapps Farm Railway Museum in Essex. Author

16 Fenland crossings

Part of the Fens of southern Lincolnshire are known as Holland and, between Spalding and King's Lynn, is a particularly flat area reclaimed from the sea. One of the first lines in this area ran from Spalding to Holbeach and was opened in 1858. It was extended to Sutton Bridge in 1862 and King's Lynn, for freight, by 1864. The flat nature of the land resulted in numerous road level crossings. These were sometimes provided near operational signalboxes or at stations, and a sprinkling of road bridges were also provided, but the sheer number of road crossings were to be a heavy financial burden in later years as wages increased and traffic declined.

The railway formed an important feature of the Fen towns in this area and associated with the railway were a number of railway named, rather than owned, hotels and public houses. The Station Hotel at Holbeach still retains its station title, though the station itself closed to passengers in February 1959. This public house was once run by my great-grandfather, of whom on reflection I am rather envious, running a pub beside a station; what more could one want from life? Such hostelries have survived the closure of the railway, but when lines were open they were a hive of activity associated with rail traffic. Both passengers and station staff, the latter often being well-known

Left: Staff pose at Holbeach station at the turn of the century. Note the absence of a substantial platform canopy at this station. Agricultural produce was the main freight traffic at such stations.
Author's Collection

Below: A similar view of Holbeach station taken in August 1994. Remarkably little change is evident in spite of passenger services having been withdrawn for almost four decades. Author

Left: Sutton Bridge station photographed with a train awaiting
to depart for King's Lynn.
Judging by the passengers waiting to travel towards Spalding
the train on the right could probably be waiting for one to come
off the single-line swing bridge
located just east of the station.
Real Photographs Co

Below: Holbeach station 1932.
Crown Copyright

personalities in the community, tested the brews.

Although the M&GN did not pass through areas of precipitous geography, there being only one tunnel at Bourne, it was forced to cross a number of rivers by substantial bridges including that at Sutton Bridge over the River Nene, at King's Lynn over the River Ouse, at Potter Heigham over the River Thurne and over Breydon Water at Yarmouth. It is said that the need to repair the bridge over the River Ouse at King's Lynn expedited the end of the route.

The community of Sutton Bridge apart from lending its arms to the M&GN crest derives its name, per-haps not unexpectedly, from a bridge over the River Nene at this point. The first swing road bridge, to allow sailing ships along the Nene to Wisbech, was opened in 1850 and the street pattern clearly indicates where an earlier bridge was located, a little way north of the present bridge.

When later the railway came to this area, the 10-mile Lynn and Sutton Bridge section was perhaps

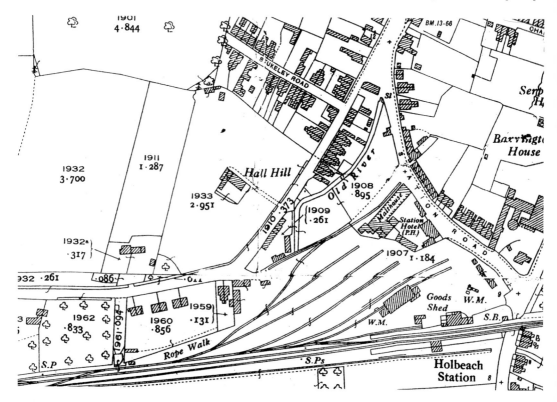

Right: An ex-LMS 0-6-0 crosses the single-track swing bridge over the River Nene at Sutton Bridge with a return excursion from Yarmouth Beach on 9 August 1958. F. Church

Below right: Lines leading to Sutton Bridge 1931. Crown Copyright

Below: The swing bridge at Sutton Bridge viewed after the opening of the former railway side of the bridge to road traffic as this view taken in July 1968 shows. Note the height restriction. T. G. Hepburn

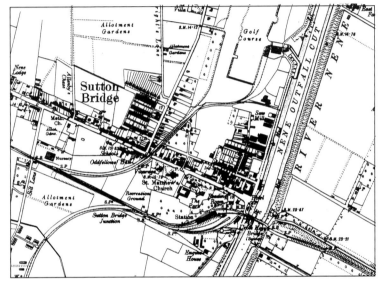

a little unfortunate in that it was forced to cross both the River Ouse and the River Nene on its route from King's Lynn to Sutton Bridge. In crossing the River Ouse the railway was able to build a five-span lattice girder bridge as this was to the south of King's Lynn docks and on a section of the river not used by substantial craft.

At Sutton Bridge the road bridge was at first adapted and widened for the railway also to operate over it by 1864. The present Cross Keys bridge was opened in July 1897 and provided a single track for both road and rail traffic. It is of a steel girder type with a considerable swing span of 176ft. It was designed by Mr J. McDonald and for a number of years tolls were collected for road traffic crossing the bridge. Until relatively recently the bridge was opened and closed by a system of hydraulics. The housing for this equipment was located some distance from the bridge itself and although unused, the buildings housing this equipment still remain.

The line from Sutton Bridge eastward over the bridge closed to all traffic in February 1959. This was

Above: The swing bridge at Sutton Bridge in August 1994 — note that the central control tower and strengthening arches over the roads have been raised to allow high vehicles to pass through the bridge. Author

Left: Part of the turning mechanism and defences to prevent shipping running into the bridge, viewed from near the bridge control tower. Author

Above: A view towards the former Sutton Bridge station area from the swing bridge in August 1994. Author

Right: The attractive brass hydraulic gauge in the control tower located on the swing bridge at Sutton Bridge. The bridge is no longer turned by a system of hydraulics and the equipment has been rendered redundant. Nonetheless, being a listed structure, such equipment can only be removed by consent. Author

an early rationalisation and much was made of this at the time. After some deliberation the railway track on the bridge was converted into a second roadway and the bridge, which is a listed structure, remains essentially unchanged since its construction. The control tower located on the bridge retains much of its Victorian equipment, although it was raised in height to accommodate road traffic. A footpath has been added, but much of a railway flavour remains, including the old railway oil lamps that act as reserve warning to shipping approaching the bridge should the later fitted electric lamps fail. The bridge remains in use as a roadway and almost the entire line from Sutton Bridge to King's Lynn has been converted into a roadway.

Union with Cambridge

Cambridge, with its University, colleges, court-yards and churches, is one of the most attractive towns in England. At a crossing point on the River Cam it has long been a route centre and transport focus. The University did not exactly welcome the railway, imposing restrictions on Sunday use and preventing a town centre branch from being constructed. Nevertheless the town did become the nucleus of railway activity and a fine station was built incorporating the arms of the colleges on its front arcade.

Although Cambridge station effectively had only

Left: Class E4 2-4-0 No 62785 approaches Barnwell Junction on a stopping train from Mildenhall to Cambridge in August 1953. P. J. Lynch

Below: The 4.21pm Cambridge-Mildenhall train caught at Burwell station on the last day of passenger services, 16 June 1962. L. Sandler

one main platform, it would not be wrong to say that eight lines once radiated from the town. Running in a clockwise direction the lines served Hunstanton, Mildenhall, Newmarket, Haverhill, London, Royston, Oxford and St Ives. Not all are lost lines, but some currently out of use are considered below.

Mildenhall

The line to Mildenhall served what was once an inland port town linked to the River Ouse. The GER's

Above: Class 4MT No 43149, heading a M&GN Railway Preservation Society special on 26 May 1962, passes through Fordham en route for Mildenhall. D. Rees

Below: Fordham station photographed in September 1994; part of the buildings remain, albeit in residential use. The Ely-Bury St Edmunds line still passes through the station. Author

19¼-mile line from Barnwell Junction to Mildenhall opened to Fordham Junction, on the Ely-Bury line, in June 1884 and throughout to Mildenhall by April 1885. The line was always somewhat of a backwater, but this said, was important during World War 2 in serving the large Mildenhall air base. In July 1958 DMUs were introduced on the route, but patronage did not increase significantly and passenger services were ultimately withdrawn in June 1962. The air base was still in operation, but it was usually found that Shippea Hill on the main line provided a more convenient service.

Freight continued until July 1964 when all but a section between Fordham Junction and Burwell was closed entirely; this section itself closed in April 1965 and Fordham station in September of the same year.

Left: The 18.18 Cambridge-St
Ives train leaves Histon on
Monday 20 April 1970.
J. Vaughan

Below: A similar view of Histon
station taken in September
1994. The overgrown track
remains in situ and there are
strong hopes of a revival. Author

Today the substantial Mildenhall station remains and the site very well preserves the station buildings and grounds. Bottisham & Lode station also remains as does Fordham, although both are rather less well maintained than Mildenhall.

St Ives

The 14-mile line to St Ives branched off the main line to the north of Cambridge at Chesterton Junction and was opened in August 1847 by the ECR. The line continued westward to Godmanchester and was opened, albeit by a different railway company, the Ely & Huntingdon Railway, the same day. In February 1848

a link from St Ives to March was completed.

The link from St Ives to Godmanchester, which had been extended to Huntingdon (East) and Kettering was the first to close in June 1959, whilst economies were made to the remaining sections from St Ives to March and to Cambridge in 1967.

Unfortunately this was not able to save St Ives and all remaining passenger services closed in October 1970. Mineral traffic from Fen Drayton to the main line at Cambridge line survived until 1992.

Only the former Station Hotel remains at St Ives and is now used as an office. Nevertheless, the track

Above: The substantial interior and extensive number of levers at St Ives signalbox give an indication of the once considerable importance of this junction. This view was taken in August 1952. British Railways

Right: St Ives station seen on Friday 2 October 1970 during the final week of passenger trains on the route from Cambridge to March. This view shows a DMU awaiting with the 09.44 departure to Cambridge whilst a Type 2 No 5532 shunts freight. The abandoned platform to the left of the photograph was where trains once ran through to Huntingdon and Kettering. G. R. Mortimer

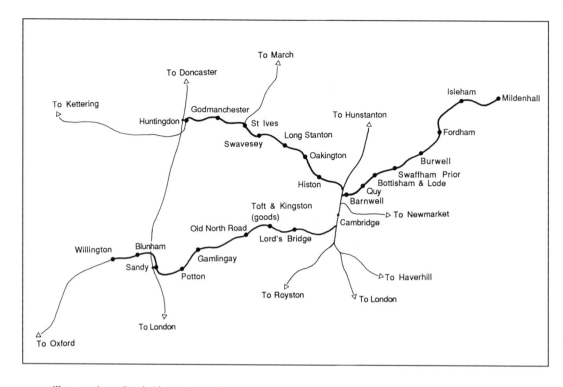

To March
To Doncaster
To Kettering
Isleham — Mildenhall
Godmanchester
To Hunstanton
Huntingdon
St Ives
Long Stanton
Fordham
Swavesey
Oakington
Burwell
Swaffham Prior
Histon
Bottisham & Lode
Quy
Barnwell
To Newmarket
Toft & Kingston
(goods)
Old North Road
Cambridge
Lord's Bridge
Willington
Blunham
Sandy
Gamlingay
To Haverhill
Potton
To London
To Royston
To London
To Oxford

was still extant from Cambridge as far as Fen Drayton in 1994 and may well in the future have a new lease of life. Local authorities, looking at ways of relieving congestion in Cambridge, have widespread support for reopening the line from St Ives through the Swavesey, Long Stanton, Oakington and Histon commuting areas to Cambridge. Future long term plans even consider reinstatement of the line between St Ives and Huntingdon.

Left: A similar view (see previous page) of the St Ives station area taken in September 1994. The building in the background is the former Station Hotel, the only railway associated building remaining at St Ives station. Author

Oxbridge

The line from Cambridge to Oxford developed in a number of sections. The 21¼-mile intermediate section from Cambridge to Sandy incorporated the route of the earlier Sandy & Potton line which had been privately opened to freight in June 1857 and to passengers in April of the following year. The extended

Above: The 4.55pm Cambridge-Kettering train enters Huntingdon East on 1 September 1954 hauled by 2-6-0 No 46403. Ian Allan Library

Below: A 'Black Five' No 45379 heads a westbound train through Gamlingay station. J. Spencer Gilks

Top left: The ticket office at Potton, together with the former Eastern Region name signs and much of the station, still remained in 1994. Author

Top right: A view taken from a Cambridge-Oxford train at Gamlingay station on 5 September 1964. Author

Below left: Willington station photographed on 5 September 1964. This station once marked the end of the Eastern Region section of the Cambridge-Oxford route before the line continued westward into the London Midland Region. Author

Opposite top: Over 30 years later at Willington in 1994 the Poplar trees have been felled and replanted whilst the route of the former railway line was being used as a cycle way. Author

Opposite bottom: Timetable 1955

route to Cambridge opened in 1862. The line continued to be extended and in the end became an important 76½-mile cross country link between the two university towns of Cambridge and Oxford.

The line was run by the LNWR which gave that railway access to Cambridge, and later the route became part of the LMS. On Nationalisation, however, the ER ran the line as far as Willington some four miles east of Bedford, after which the Royal Blue of the ER gave way to the maroon of the LMR. The route ran for many years without fundamental change. In 1955 the line was selected to be part of an

upgraded long distance route and the Bletchley flyover was built, but almost as soon as it was completed the idea was dropped and decline set in. In 1959 DMUs were introduced and, although a few of the intermediate stations had been closed over the years, in 1963 total closure of the route was proposed. This was vigorously opposed, but the line finally closed between Bedford and Cambridge in January 1968. Of all the lines closed in the area there has been continued pressure for the reopening of the Bedford-Sandy section of this former route which would give a useful connection between the Midland and East Coast main lines. Today part of this section is used as a cycleway, but as the years pass by the prospect of reopening becomes all the more difficult.

Table 36						CAMBRIDGE and MILDENHALL						
		Week Days only							**Week Days only**			
Miles		am	am	pm	pm	pm	Miles		am	am	pm	pm
	6 London (L'pool St) dep	4 24	8A27	12 5	24	4 36	4 27		Mildenhall .. .. dep	7 35	11 49	..	5 40	7 40	..
	12 „ (King's C.) „	....	7 ..	..2 5	....	....	1	Worlington Golf Links Halt	7 39	11 53	....	5 44	7 44	..
							4	Isleham	7 46	12 0	..	5 51	5 51	..
—	Cambridge .. .. dep	6 28	10 23	4 27	6 2	6 13	7½	Fordham.......... { arr	7 53	12 6	..	5 57	7 57	..
1½	Barnwell...........		10 27	4 31					{ dep	7 54	12 8	..	5 58	7 58	..
2½	Fen Ditton Halt.. ..	..	10 30	4 34			10	Exning Road Halt	8 1	12 15	....			
4½	Quy.................	..	10 36	4 40			10½	Burwell	8 4	12 18	....			
6	Bottisham and Lode ..	..	10 40	4 44			12½	Swaffhamprior...........	8 8	12 22	....			
8	Swaffhamprior.............		10 45	4 49			14½	Bottisham and Lode ..	..	8 13	12 27	..		
10	Burwell	..	10 50	4 54			16½	Quy.................	8 17	12 31	....			
10½	Exning Road Halt		10 53	4 57			18½	Fen Ditton Halt	8 22	12 36	..			
13½	Fordham .. .. { arr	7 0	11 0	5 3			19	Barnwell.................	8 25	12 40	....			
	{ dep	7 4	11 6	5 7	6 51	7 4	20½	Cambridge .. .. arr	8 30	12 48	..	6 47	8 39	..
16½	Isleham	..	..7 12	11 14	5 15	6 59	7 12							
19½	Worlington Golf Links Halt	....	11 21	5 22	7 6	7 19	78½	12 London (King's C.) arr	....	10 0 57	..			
20½	Mildenhall .. .. arr	7 21	11 24	5 25	7 9	7 22	76½	6 „ (L'pool St) „	9F53	2 31	..	8 40	9C53	..

18 **Loss at the races**

The first recorded horse race was held at Newmarket in 1619 and soon the town became the racing capital of England. Both the town and later

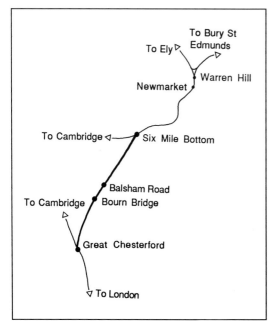

the railways were anxious to provide services for racegoers. The 17½-mile Newmarket & Chesterford Railway connected those towns and opened its line in 1848, providing a direct service from Newmarket to London. A branch was also eventually provided from Six Mile Bottom, then called Westley, to Cambridge. The terminus built at Newmarket was a very fine structure but, as with the unhappy end of the railway company that built it, was destined not to survive.

There were also plans to extend the line to Thetford, thus providing a direct route from London to Norwich via Newmarket. The Eastern Counties Railway (ECR) shareholders became increasingly concerned about this potential competition with their own line via Cambridge. Consequently they managed to take over the Newmarket & Chesterford Railway, increasing its operating charges to the extent that in June 1850 the original railway from Great Chesterford to Newmarket was forced to close. However, after much criticism the original line was reopened. Shortly after, in October 1851, the Cambridge branch opened from Six Mile Bottom and that from Great Chesterford to the junction at Six Mile Bottom was again closed, but this time it never reopened.

Traces of the old line, including crossing keepers' houses, can still be seen to this day, almost one and a half centuries after closure. The route, together with

Opposite below: The extraordinary single storey façade of the old station at Newmarket embellished by paired Ionic columns with the entablature projecting over them. The soft sandstone was in poor condition and in the early 1980s the station was demolished, although the contractor salvaged two of the columns and these remain in a local garden.
Suffolk Record Office, RCHME Crown Copyright

Right: The site of Warren Hill station at Newmarket. Unused since World War 2, the former platforms were located to the left of the remaining railway line shown in this photograph. Author

Below: The railway side of the old station at Newmarket was in complete contrast to the ornate frontage, being entirely functional.
Suffolk Record Office, RCHME Crown Copyright

Bourn Bridge and Balsham Road stations, must have been one of the earliest substantial closures in the region. Powers to abandon the line were eventually obtained in 1858 and the route was dismantled. Its closure resulted in the distance from London to Newmarket being increased by some 7½ miles.

In April 1854 an extension from Newmarket ran east to Bury St Edmunds. In order not to disturb racehorse training, the new through line passed under the town in a tunnel some 1,099yd long, the longest on the GER. The northern end of this tunnel, at Warren Hill, was close to the main racecourse and in 1885 a

terminal station was provided here especially for race-goers. Heavy excursion traffic used this station on race days. During World War 2 a hospital train was based at the station and on occasions even the royal train.

In 1902 a new through station was opened. Warren Hill remained in use, but the old terminal station, which had been linked to low level platforms immedi-ately at the tunnel entrance, was closed, although the terminal continued to operate as a freight depot. It was extensively employed during the bloodstock sales, with shunting also being carried out by horses. Nevertheless a general decline in freight developed in the 1960s and the old station was closed in 1967. It was a most attractive building with an astonishing ornate frontage, looking like some Baroque

Orangery. It was indeed described at the time of closure as one of the best buildings in Newmarket. However, following much rumour and false hopes of a reprieve, a viable new use for the building could not be found. Sadly the soft sandstone frontage was in such a poor state of repair that in 1981 the station was demolished.

Passenger services were not resumed to Warren Hill station after World War 2, whilst a connecting western spur to the Ely-Bury line closed in September 1965. Unlike the ornate old terminal, the station at Warren Hill was in complete contrast. A ramp led from staff housing to a long island platform where rather plain station facilities were provided. Today very little remains at the station itself, but the Newmarket-Bury line still passes next to the site.

The 1902 station that replaced the original terminal remains open, but the buildings are in private use. This was not before the down side structures were destroyed by fire and the up side platform canopy destroyed by BR. The station became an unstaffed halt in 1967. There was an outcry at that time when the six staff to be made redundant were given new uniforms! Today, one of the long platforms remains, with some shelters similar to those on bus routes being in sharp contrast to the elegance of the original station. Part of the station area has been used for housing, although a condition of sale was to provide improved parking at the station, because in spite of the many losses, happily lines still serve Newmarket.

19 Saved by the bells

Until the 17th century, when they were drained on a large scale, the Fens were a difficult and dangerous area to travel across. Once a year the bells of St John's at Peterborough peal at the request of Matthew Wyldbore, a former MP of the city (and distant relation) who died in 1781. A bequest he made produces £5 a year for the ringers on the anniversary of his death. The bells once guided him home when he was lost in the Fens in the fog. In later years the bells have rung over many other losses in the area, not least those of the railways.

The fortunes of Peterborough were transformed with the coming of the railway and the London & North Western, Great Northern, Great Eastern, M&GN and Midland railways all served the city. The Great Northern had a station called Cowgate, although this was later renamed North. The Midland also had, for a short time between 1858 and 1866, a station known as Crescent. The Great Eastern

Below: An almost brand-new English Electric Type 4 No D273 passes Peterborough North station with a Hull-King's Cross train on 3 October 1960. Although the East Coast main line is unlikely ever to feature as a lost line, Peterborough North station was subsequently to be completely demolished and the tracks through it realigned for high speed running. Yet the Great Northern Hotel to the right of the photograph remains almost as originally constructed. P. Wells

Bottom: LMS compound No 41097 pulls into Peterborough East station with a train from Rugby in June 1954. Although most of the buildings have subsequently been demolished, tracks still run through the site and the line remains open. R. E. Vincent

Right: Whereas the Midland's Crescent station at Peterborough survived for only a very short time the name lived on in Crescent shops as shown in this view taken on 23 August 1982. P. Waszak

Below: The wonderful stone Jacobean-style station at Wansford was built in 1845 and beautifully designed by J. W. Livock. Hopefully, the building is likely to have a secure long-term future in association with the Nene Valley Railway. Author

Railway ran to the city and provided its own station, Peterborough East. However, the London & North Western Railway, which ran via the Nene Valley from Rugby and Northampton, together with the M&GN and later the Midland Railway shared the North and East stations.

Peterborough East station closed in June 1966 and is now largely demolished. The station on the East Coast main line, formerly Peterborough North, remains open although the original GNR buildings have been demolished. However, all is not lost for

beside the North station is the Great Northern Hotel, designed for the GNR by Henry Goddard in 1849. Unlike the adjoining station, the hotel still retains its original name and many of its original features.

Travelling west from Peterborough you soon ran out of the Eastern Region; nevertheless one such line that ran in the ER as far as Thorpe was in the Nene Valley. The line formed part of an early 43½-mile route from Northampton to Peterborough, via Wansford, constructed by the London & Birmingham Railway and opened in June 1845. Later the LNWR took over

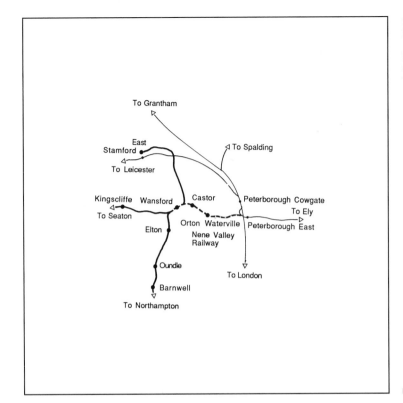

To Grantham

East
Stamford

To Leicester

To Spalding

Kingscliffe   Wansford   Castor   Peterborough Cowgate

To Seaton   To Ely

Elton   Orton Waterville   Peterborough East

Nene Valley
Railway

Oundle

Barnwell

To Northampton

To London

Below: The interior of Stamford
East station pictured on 2 March
1957, the last day of services.
Ex-GNR Class C12 No 67376 has
arrived with the 3.15pm service
from Essendine. P. Wells

the route and opened a line west from Wansford to Seaton (see the LMR volume in the 'Lost Lines' series) in November 1879, whilst a GNR link also opened from Wansford to a station at Stamford East in August 1867.

Stamford is celebrated for its stone architecture and townscape, to which the railways also contributed. Although the branch from Wansford to Stamford closed in July 1929 fortunately the Tudor styled station at Stamford East, built to reflect nearby Burghley House, remains. Wansford station itself was the next to close in July 1957, but again the impressive stone built Jacobean-styled station, once located on the Great North Road, remains. The original route to Northampton closed to passengers in May 1964, the link to Seaton closed two years later and the line through Wansford to all freight by 1972.

Yet this was not the end of the story. Today the Nene Valley Railway runs from its new station in Peterborough, via Orton Mere, to Wansford station

Above: The stone elegance of Stamford East station, which was built in 1856, can be seen in this photograph taken a few months before closure. T. Rounthwaite

Below: After closure the beautiful buildings at Stamford East remained in a derelict condition, as this view taken on 2 January 1965 shows. P. Wells

and Yarwell Junction, providing a very attractive route along the River Nene on this former Eastern Region section of the longer line. This section of line was saved by the bell thanks to Peterborough Development Corporation in 1973. Today locomotives and coaches from 10 countries have also been saved for use on the route which can accommodate the wider continental loading gauge. This and the surrounding countryside are such that the line has been used for many film and TV locations, supposedly located in other parts of Europe or set in earlier times.

20 The Lincolnshire coastlines

There are about some 90 miles of low sandy Lincolnshire coastline which, before the advent of the railway, embraced at one time just a scattering of fishing villages such as Skegness, Sutton-le-Marsh, Mablethorpe and indeed at one time even Grimsby. The first railway in the area was the 45½-mile East Lincolnshire Railway (ELR) which opened its line from Grimsby to Louth in March 1848 and southwards to Firsby and Boston by October of that year. The line was built primarily to tap the rich agricultural land of the Lincoln Marsh, between the Wolds and the coast, rather than to exploit the coast itself.

Left: The town of Louth boasts the highest parish church steeple in the country. It also boasted the best station buildings on the Great Northern Railway. Unfortunately the beautiful Jacobean station buildings, dating from 1848, soon fell into disrepair on the closure of the line through the town, as this view taken on 29 June 1977 shows. S. Creer

Below: After years lying derelict the station is gradually being converted into residential units, although this new use was some way off completion when this view was taken in September 1994. Author

Left: Mablethorpe station during what appears to be a quiet period in the summer, but which on careful examination shows that considerable activity is being planned, both on the track and by the station staff. J. Cupit

Below: The 'Jolly Fisherman' poster for Skegness boasted of the town's bracing air and became nationally famous. A substantial publicity campaign was launched by the LNER for other East Coast destinations and this poster for Mablethorpe took on a different theme, highlighting the delights of the sandy beach. Courtesy NRM

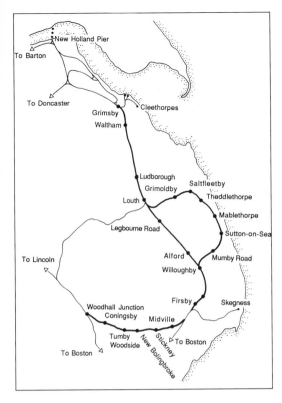

Below: The DMU in this view is the 15.52 to Willoughby from Mablethorpe. The unit ran round and back into the station. The direct line in the far distance beyond Mablethorpe to Louth had been discontinued when this photograph was taken on 9 July 1969. J. A. M. Vaughan

At the same time as the railways were developing, sea bathing was becoming increasingly popular and the golden shelving Lincolnshire sands were ideal for such purposes. To the west lay the growing population of the industrial Midlands. This combination inevitably led to proposals to make this coast more accessible by train and a number of lines were built to feed traffic to the coast. The Louth & East Coast Railway opened a 12-mile line from Louth to Mablethorpe in October 1877. This connected in October 1886 with the 9¾-mile Willoughby & Sutton Railway to form a 22½-mile coastal loop line off the ELR from the handsome Jacobean-styled station at Louth to the station at Willoughby. A line was also extended from Firsby via Wainfleet to Skegness where a substantial station was built in correct

anticipation of the growing holiday traffic.

Other lines ran from Boston to Lincoln and Nottingham and to other Midland destinations, all of which allowed the growing industrial towns easy access to the coast. Thus it was that the Lincolnshire coast became a huge attraction, in particular Skegness, but also both Mablethorpe and Sutton-on-Sea. A vast summer excursion traffic built up, with lines and stations being used to capacity at peak times.

Above: A tramway once ran to the coast, but was soon put out of business after the completion of the railway. This view of Tramway Crossing between Mablethorpe and Sutton-on-Sea, taken on 19 September 1970, recalls the long closed tramway system. S. C. Dent

Left: The site of Tramway Crossing could still clearly be identified in September 1994, as this similar view shows. Author

Right: This view of Mumby Road station signalbox and wooden freight shed was taken from a DMU heading to Willoughby on 6 August 1964. *Author*

Below: Mumby Road station pictured on 9 August 1969. The line through the station had been singled and only some trains called at the dilapidated station at this time. By 1994 the buildings viewed here had gone, but the station house and one of the original oil lamps still remained. *J. A. M. Vaughan*

Although the seaside towns themselves grew, traffic was of a marked seasonal nature and in winter the lines would be far less used. Diesel trains were introduced in 1955, but little real economies were made both to signalling and in automating the many road crossings in the flat coastal area. The change in holiday trends and the growth in car traffic also played their part in the decline. The area has seen a catalogue of closures. The Louth-Mablethorpe line closed in December 1960 thus ending the coastal loop service. The line from Mablethorpe to Willoughby survived 10 years further until October 1970 when the

main East Lincolnshire line from Boston to Spalding and from Firsby to Grimsby also closed, together with the line from Bellwater Junction to Lincoln Central although freight survived between Grimsby and Louth until 1980.

The railways were thus decimated in east Lincolnshire, but not without a vigorous fight by the local authorities who were concerned about rural depopulation and the isolation resulting from closure. Thus it was that although there was pressure also to

Right: A similar view of Tumby Woodside in September 1994. The end of the platform is just visible in the dense undergrowth. Author

Below: The 15.22 Firsby-Lincoln train stops at the all-wooden platforms at Midville on 9 August 1969. Although not shown on the timetable, the train worked through to Sheffield. Again of note was the extensive use of wood in the construction of station platforms on the Bellwater Junction-Woodhall Junction, Kirkstead line. J. A. M. Vaughan

close the line to Skegness, this has fortunately survived, although services, rather like its pier, are on a much reduced scale. Many of the station buildings remain. Louth station, the most attractive on the whole of the former GNR and a listed building has been saved. Italianate Alford and the distinctive barge-boards on the gables of Mumby Road and Sutton-on-Sea also remain. The station at Legbourne Road has been preserved as a museum, as once was Burgh-le-Marsh. There are plans to reopen the route from Louth northwards via Ludborough to near Grimsby as a preserved line.

Perhaps any reference to the Lincolnshire coast would be incomplete without mention of that part which becomes the Humber estuary. Prior to the opening of the Humber bridge the railways played an

Above: Firsby acted as an important junction for Skegness. It boasted an overall roof and numerous ex-Great Northern somersault signals, as this view taken on 7 February 1970 shows. M. C. Barker

Below: Today only part of the station house remains at Firsby, as this photograph taken in August 1994 shows. Author

Above: Class K2 No 61729 passing Firsby East Junction with an express comprising a mix of coaches for Skegness. The Boston-Grimsby line can be seen in the background, whilst the spur to the right was for Firsby. This view was taken in the late 1950s. P. Wells

Below: Class 47 locomotive No 1940 also comes off the south curve at Firsby East with the 08.25 Manchester Piccadilly-Skegness train on 29 August 1970, again with a mix of liveried coaches. Today the curve to Skegness remains, but all the connecting spurs and other lines have gone. J. S. Hancock

Left: Derby-built DMU units form the 18.00 for Cleethorpes about to depart from a derelict looking New Holland Pier station on 24 May 1980. B. Morrison

Below: This view of New Holland Pier signalbox and the general dilapidated state of the Pier station was taken on 30 August 1980. Once the Humber road bridge opened, passenger services to New Holland Pier were discontinued in June 1981. P. Harris

important part in providing connections between Hull and Grimsby. Connections across the water were provided by a branch off the Sheffield to Grimsby line between Brocklesby and Habrough stations to a pier at New Holland. Here ferries once ran across the Humber to Hull Corporation Pier. There still remains a service to New Holland, but passenger services to the Pier station succumbed, together with the Humber ferries, not unexpectedly, in June 1981 with the opening of the Humber road bridge.

21 Lost links with Lincoln

Lincoln, the county town of Lincolnshire, has a most imposing cathedral and remains an important market and administrative centre. Being at a gap in the Lincoln Edge it became a natural focus for transport routes dating back to Roman times. After fire and earthquake the vast triple-towered cathedral was completed and in later years the railways entered the city. Many lines focused on the city and as such it developed as both an important railway and industrial centre. At one time it boasted two stations and was served by the Great Northern, Midland, Great Central and Great Northern & Great Eastern Joint Line.

The Dukeries Route

The Lancashire, Derbyshire & East Coast Railway had aspirations of a trans-England route from the Manchester Ship Canal to a new east coast port at Sutton-on-Sea, running via Lincoln. In fact only a 39½-mile section between Chesterfield Market Place and Lincoln Central was ever built, together with a number of later link lines including one to Mansfield. The central section of line from Chesterfield to Lincoln opened in March 1897 and passed through that part of Sherwood Forest known as the Dukeries. Consequently the railway hoped to build on tourist traffic, but the majority of its income came from coal traffic. The line became part of the GCR in 1907.

The east-west route of the line encountered some difficult terrain, having to cross the River Trent and associated flood plain near High Marnham, and opening of the line was delayed by problems with the construction of the 1 mile 864yd Bolsover Tunnel. This continued to cause difficulties, because of the shale deposits through which it ran and because of mining

Left: This view of Chesterfield Market Place looking west, with the imposing town hall in the background, was taken after the closure of the station to passengers in 1951, but prior to the station's complete closure for freight. J. Cupit

Below: A similar view of the area taken in September 1994. All trace of the station has been lost under a number of developments. Author

subsidence in the area, and closure of the section between Chesterfield and Langwith came in December 1951. In later years there were few passenger trains on the remaining section and the whole route closed to regular passengers in September 1955, although by that time only three passenger trains called at all stations. Part of the line and Warsop, Edwinstowe and Ollerton stations remained in use for seasonal holiday traffic until September 1964 when the section east of High Marnham to Lincoln closed.

A central section from Shirebrook remained open for freight to High Marnham power station until early in 1994, when it was cut back during that year to Thoresby for regular coal traffic, although High Marnham still retains its rail facilities.

The Grantham Route

The line from Honington Junction, just east of Honington station, on the Grantham-Boston line ran for the most part along the western fringes of the limestone hills of the Lincoln Edge, through Caythorpe, Leadenham and past Welbourn, where a station was never provided, and via Waddington to Lincoln. The line was opened in April 1867 by the GNR. It was built to main line standards and provided the GNR with a more direct route from Lincoln to King's Cross. Equally it opened up an area of Jurassic

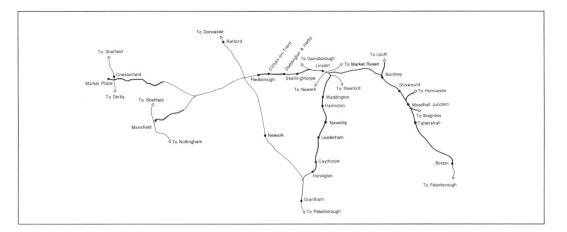

ironstone. However, although mineral trains ran for a time to Scunthorpe and Derbyshire, supplies of suitable grade ore were soon exhausted.

As the petrol engine began increasingly to replace the horse, Waddington provided a gruesome trade for this line in transporting cart horses to a nearby knacker's yard. The Waddington air base also provided some traffic, but after World War 2 decline set in. One of the problems with the line was that most local stations were located some distance away from the villages they served, the exception being Leadenham. Therefore it was no great surprise that all the intermediate stations, except Leadenham, were closed in September 1962. In addition, most of the Lincoln trains running south operated via Sleaford and Peterborough, rather than via Grantham. Economies were made to both track and signalling, but the 18¼-mile route was closed in November 1965.

Centre: The closed Caythorpe station photographed in October 1964. Trains still ran through the station from Grantham to Lincoln at this time. All but one of the intermediate stations on this line had been closed and the track and signalling simplified. Note the BR signal arm on the platform. Author

Right: By October 1982 the same station platform at Caythorpe had sprouted a young wood as this view shows. Author

The Loop Line

The Great Northern Railway made an impressive push northward in October 1848 by opening a line from Peterborough through Boston and along the course of the Witham Navigation to Lincoln. The line was part of the 'Loop', off the East Coast main line, but the development of lines, such as the East Lincolnshire line from Boston to Grimsby, and

Above: Leadenham station was a fine stone-built structure and in 1994, when this view was taken, was for sale as one of the more desirable residences in the village. Author

Left: Sincil Bank signalbox taken from a DMU approaching Lincoln from the Grantham line on 24 March 1956. Ian Allan Library

another to Lincoln itself made the 31-mile link from Boston to Lincoln somewhat of a secondary route and in later years it provided mainly a local service between Lincoln and Boston. It passed near the town of Woodhall Spa, where health-giving springs were found by chance when an abandoned coal shaft flooded into a ditch and appeared to have health giving properties for the livestock that drank the water. As a consequence a 7½-mile branch was opened by the Horncastle Railway in 1855 from Kirkstead, later renamed Woodhall Junction, to Woodhall Spa and on to Horncastle. A 21½-mile link was also finally opened in December 1876 by the Louth & Lincoln Railway and provided a link from Bardney, over the Wolds, to Louth.

All the lines, except that to Horncastle, were

Above: Tattershall Castle's medieval quadrangular tower is particularly delightful. Equally the station at Tattershall with its own distinctive tower was one of the most attractive on the loop line. In 1994 the station was in use as an art gallery where this view by Arthur Watson was available.

Right: The typical ex-GNR signal-box and crossing gates at Stixwould viewed from a DMU on 19 September 1970. S. C. Dent

eventually owned by the GNR, whilst they also provided a late link in 1913 from Woodhall Junction via Midville, the Kirkstead and Little Steeping line, which enabled direct access from Lincoln to Skegness. The new route crossed a relatively remote area and the line closed soon after opening between 1915 and 1923 due to coal shortages. The route over the Wolds from Bardney to Louth closed to passengers in November 1951 and completely by 1956, whilst that to

Horncastle closed to passengers in September 1954. Part of the Loop from Boston to Woodhall Junction closed in June 1963, whilst the link from Bellwater Junction via Midville to Woodhall Junction and on to Lincoln closed to passengers in October 1970. Freight to Horncastle lasted a few months longer, but the Bardney sugar beet factory retained rail services from Lincoln until 1983.

Above: The 16.00 Lincoln Central-Tumby Woodside local approaching Bardney on 26 September 1970. In this case the all-wooden signalbox, which is beginning to look a little the worse for wear, seems to have required a little strengthening over the years. J. S. Hancock

Right: After closure to passenger services some sugar beet freight remained at the Lincoln end of the Fens Loop and a freight line special rail tour was run to a remarkably complete Bardney station on 6 September 1980. The station has since been dismantled for future use by Railworld. R. King

22 Pass over the Pennines

The 13-mile line from Sheffield Victoria to Penistone was part of the Eastern Region's contribution to the eventually electrified 41¼-mile line between Sheffield and Manchester. This really was a wonderful line, not only in terms of Pennine scenery, with the sombre and massive interlocking hills of millstone grit, but also because it was electrified to very advanced principles in that trains descending on the line returned power to the system instead of dissipating it in heat through the brakes.

The line once formed part of the Great Central Railway's main line from Marylebone to Manchester, with the Sheffield-Manchester section opening in 1845, and climbing to a summit of almost 1,000ft in crossing the Pennines. Although for many years a main passenger route, freight, in the form of coal, was

Left: This view of extensive activity at the west end of Sheffield Victoria station was taken at the turn of the century. Note the passenger lift and subway in the centre of the view. Locomotive Publishing Co

Below left: The same subway at Sheffield Victoria station seen in September 1994, one of the few surviving remains of the station. Author

the mainstay of the line, both from Sheffield and from Wath-upon-Dearne marshalling yard up Worsbrough incline to Penistone. Such was the volume of traffic on these routes that the LNER considered electrification the best way of resolving congestion on these heavy gradients over the Pennines to Manchester.

Electrification over the Pennines faced a number of setbacks. First, soon after contracts were let World War 2 broke out and work came to an end. Second, the condition of the two single bore tunnels dating back to 1845 through the Pennines at Woodhead were worse than expected and the construction of a brand new tunnel had to be undertaken. This three-mile 66yd bore added some £4.25 million to the cost of upgrading the route and delayed the opening.

The electrification was at 1,500V dc and electric locomotives were produced at Gorton Works for use on the line. They were of two types, four-axle (Bo-Bo) 1,868hp and six-axle (Co-Co) 2,700hp locomotives. The latter were capable of speeds of up to 90mph. As it happened, the first one built was sent over to The Netherlands after World War 2 due to the shortage of workable equipment because of war damage.

Left: The approach to Sheffield Victoria station pictured on 29 November 1969. The clock tower of the modernised station has since gone, but the hotel at the far left of the view remains. I. S. Carr

Centre left: Although almost all of Sheffield Victoria station has been demolished, the Royal Victoria Hotel, opened in 1862, remains as this view taken in September 1994 shows. The hotel, as with so many other railway hotels, once had its own direct link to the station. Author

Opposite top: The final stages of work on electrification are carried out at Sheffield Victoria station in the summer of 1954. In the interests of health and safety let's hope the 'B1' No 61211 is not rushing through the station at high speed! P. N. Coldwell

Opposite bottom: The Great Central rail tour leaves Sheffield Victoria headed by 'B1s' Nos 61131 and 61173 on 1 September 1961. J. Clarke

Below: Sheffield 1924. Crown Copyright

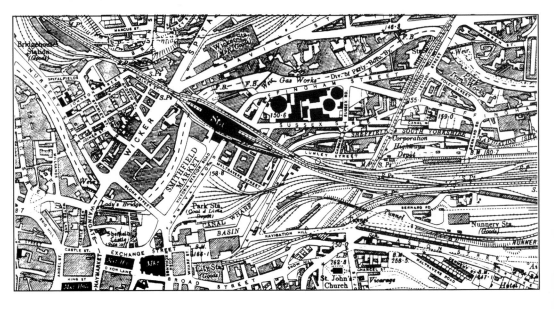

The Dutch called it Tommy which became its official name on its return to England. The route eventually opened for electric trains in June 1954, some 18 years after the first contracts were let and passenger train times were dramatically cut over this heavily graded route. My diary records being vigorously hauled up the fierce gradients from Sheffield — with Pandora in charge — with the greatest of ease.

Such was the period of gestation between planning and opening that by the time trains were running circumstances had changed. The line was no longer a main route to Sheffield and Manchester and this remaining Pennine section of the ex-GCR did not connect, without reversal, to Sheffield Midland station. The route began to look increasingly isolated with the closure of much of the former GCR main line from

Above: Class 76 electric locomotive No 76029 leads a double-headed freight train through the disused platforms at Penistone on 12 November 1980. S. Edge

Left: A similar view looking towards Manchester at Penistone in September 1994. Author

Left: The first train to traverse the eastern side of the Woodhead line since closure did so on 26 October 1983 when Class 20 No 20056 propelled two flat wagons and a brake van from Penistone to Dunford Bridge. The train is seen arriving at Dunford. The wagons were left at the station to be loaded with recovered materials. R. Kaye

Below: They certainly did recover materials. This is a similar view of Dunford Bridge taken in September 1994. Only the road overbridge, platform edge and a few immovable concrete items remain. It is hard to imagine that at one time Dunford Bridge accommodated 1,100 men involved with the construction of the new Woodhead Tunnel. Author

London to Sheffield. The electrical equipment was becoming life expired in some respects and certainly was beginning to look dated compared with later electrification schemes, being 1,500V dc compared to 25kV ac which was to become the norm on other electrified lines.

Arguments for closure of passenger services rested partly on the diversion of services to other lines, but also that there were difficulties in incorporating fast passenger trains within the intensive freight services. Sadly almost as soon as passenger services were withdrawn over the trans-Pennine section in January 1970, freight decline began to accelerate and in 1972 seven of the electric locomotives — the Co-Co Class EM2s — were sold to The Netherlands. There was a change in both the number and location of

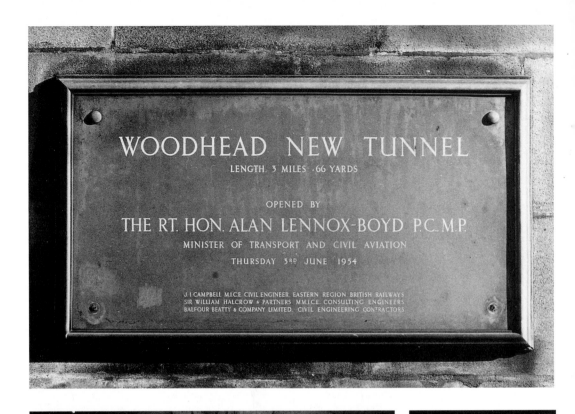

Above: This plaque photographed in 1964 on the western portal of Woodhead Tunnel speaks for itself. J. Clarke

Left: An interior view of the new Woodhead Tunnel as it neared completion in 1953. The 21in-thick concrete horseshoe-shaped tunnel has a height of 20ft 7¼in and a maximum width of 27ft. The tunnel was fitted with electric lighting and had one 16ft-diameter 450ft-deep shaft, making it one of the most substantial modern abandoned civil engineering works in the world. British Railways

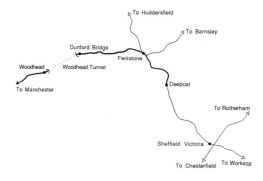

collieries using the route. As a consequence the line was only being used to about a third of its capacity in the late 1970s, which due to increasing recession at this time reduced to less than a quarter of its freight capacity in a very short time. In particular the rationalisation of collieries meant that motive power had to be changed from diesel to electric traction for many of the longer trans-Pennine journeys which added to the overall costs of using this route. Consideration was given to renewing the electrical equipment and locomotives, but a figure of £44 million was estimated to be required.

Thus it was that freight was withdrawn over the Woodhead route in July 1981. Nevertheless the loss of such a major electrified trans-Pennine route attracted national attention, not least in view of the fact that millions of pounds had been spent on the new

Left: Class B1 No 1158 heads a down express leaving Woodhead Tunnel on 27 March 1948. It can be seen from this view that considerable work remained to be completed on the electrification scheme at that time. S. Taylor

Below: English Electric Type 3 No D6748 emerges from Woodhead Tunnel with the Harwich-Liverpool boat train on 2 6 March 1967. The old tunnels can be seen to the left of the picture. The fact that the train was not electrically-hauled over this section highlights the isolation of the route in the wider network, a factor that was later to speed its demise.
K. P. Lawrence

Right: Class 76 electric locomotive No E26049 Jason approaches Penistone with the 'SLS/MLS Woodhead Rail Tour' which was returning to Manchester Piccadilly on Saturday 29 November 1969, a few weeks before closure of the line to passenger services.
I. S. Carr

Below: A narrow gauge railway line still leads into one of the old Woodhead tunnels at Dunford Bridge as the tunnel carries electricity cables under the Pennines. This view taken in September 1994 shows the eastern approach to the old tunnels, unused by main line trains for over 40 years. Author

Woodhead Tunnel which had been used for just 27 years. Objections ensured that when the route was closed for passengers in 1970 a DMU service continued to Penistone. Such was the concern at the ending of all services that pledges were given that even after closure to freight the line would remain unsold for a number of years. However, DMUs to Penistone were diverted via Barnsley in May 1983, leaving today just a freight link between Sheffield and Deepcar. Yet not all is lost: at Sheffield the Royal Victoria Hotel remains, together with a few parts of the adjoining Victoria station and the nearby beautiful ashlar stone Wicker Arches. The new Woodhead Tunnel remains unused, but one of the old ones is used to convey electricity cables under the Pennines. The line is not yet past reuse — let's hope that one day trains once again thunder through the Woodhead Tunnel.

Gricing at Grantham

The town of Grantham lies in the valley of the River Witham which necessitated tunnels being constructed through the ridges on all three lines that run out of the town. It is an attractive market town and a perfect view of St Wulfram's church, with its spectacular spire, is gained from the East Coast main line. The town contains the country's only living pub sign, a beehive, and has associations with Sir Isaac Newton and Margaret Thatcher. It has a compact and attractive shopping centre, a good market and is home to Aveling & Barford of steamroller fame.

Grantham was once proclaimed Britain's most boring town. In my view nothing could be further from the truth. In addition to its many fine qualities it has very much of transport interest. The Great North Road ran through the town, the Grantham Canal

Left: Grantham station on 3 August 1962. An 'A3' Pacific No 60065 hurries through the station with a King's Cross-Leeds relief train, whilst an 'L1' 2-6-4T No 67745 waits in the bay with the 3pm for Derby. In the far distance, on the right hand side of this view, the locomotive shed can just be seen. J. M. Rayner

Below: Grantham on 31 August 1965 — BRCW Type 3 No D 6573, with the Cliffe-Uddingstone cement train, rumbles through the station. The number is keenly spotted. C. Burton

Above: The 08.00 Aberdeen-King's Cross InterCity 125 service speeds through Grantham in January 1986. The ever-changing development on the East Coast main line is evident as the island platform buildings and canopies were being rebuilt in preparation for electrification of the route and a long-term future for the railway. A. Taylor

united the town to the River Trent and then came the Great Northern Railway. In early days the Stirling 8ft single engines would be changed at Grantham and the town developed a substantial motive power depot. The railway was prominent throughout the town. Even in my childhood I can remember waiting outside a butcher's shop only to see an endless count of engines being turned on the triangle arrangement associated with the locomotive depot. It was and still is a wonderful centre for train-spotters, or 'gricers' as they are sometimes known.

The surrounding countryside is also of great interest. Ironstone was an important local feature and an extensive network of lines built up in the area. At Harlaxton a network of steam-operated ironstone railways established in 1941 crossed the country roads until closure in 1974, although part was reopened for a short spell in 1976. At Great Gonerby extensive maltings were once served by sidings operated from a most attractive GNR signalbox. It was here that my grandparents farmed land cut by the Grantham avoiding line (one of the last sections to lose its GNR somersault signals) and the Nottingham line. As a consequence they were able to purchase for £11 masses of wooden railway fencing — which was being replaced by concrete fencing to prevent burning by sparks from steam trains, just of course as steam was being replaced by diesels!

In terms of railway interest there was and still is always something interesting to be seen, as Grantham is on a high speed stretch of the East Coast main line. I can recall an 'A4' Pacific screaming down from Stoke Tunnel, the distinctive hooter at full blast and making a spectacular sight as it stormed through the station. This was later followed by the 'Deltics', no less spectacular in their own way. Indeed once past the restriction of Grantham station, as they accelerated at full throttle, either towards Peascliffe or Stoke tunnels, the sound of their distinctive diesel engines resounded over the whole town.

Even today there is much of interest. The locomotive depot has gone, but the original Great Northern station main buildings remain. The sight and sound of a train dashing across the town today, on its numerous viaducts, bridges and embankments adds another dimension to one of the most interesting of towns. It also affirms the view that although there may well be many lost lines, railways have a great future.